HERB GARDENING
AT ITS BEST

Books by Sal Gilbertie with Larry Sheehan

Herb Gardening at Its Best   *1978*
Home Gardening at Its Best   *1977*

HERB GARDENING AT ITS BEST

Everything You Need to Know about Growing Your Favorite Herbs

SAL GILBERTIE

with Larry Sheehan

New York ATHENEUM

Garden Plans drawn by Lauren Jarrett

Plant drawings by Kristina Lynch

Atheneum
Macmillan Publishing Company
866 Third Avenue, New York, NY 10022
Collier Macmillan Canada, Inc.

Library of Congress Cataloging-in-Publication Data

Gilbertie, Sal.
  Herb gardening at its best.

Includes index.
1. Herb gardening.   I. Sheehan, Larry, joint
author.   II. Title.
SB351.H5G54   635'.7   77-23678
ISBN 0-689-70595-6

Macmillan books are available at special discounts for bulk purchases
for sales promotions, premiums, fund-raising, or educational use.
For details, contact:

Special Sales Director
Macmillan Publishing Company
866 Third Avenue
New York, NY 10022

First Atheneum Paperback Printing 1980

10   9   8   7   6   5

Printed in the United States of America

Contents

PART IV

PART V

PART I

"Quick, Learn About Herbs!"

THE WOMAN who got us launched in the business of growing herbs was known around town as the Countess.

The Countess was a remote personality with aristocratic tastes and the wealth to indulge them. She had a greenhouse built just for sunbathing on cool days. She had phones rigged up on trees throughout her estate so she could communicate with her workers without meeting them face to face.

One of her gardeners worked for her for three years without seeing her. He lost his job one day when the Countess rang him up at some tree to order three dozen rose bushes installed in a certain spot. He observed that he would also have to buy five or six yards of cow manure to plant the roses properly. She replied, "No one uses the word 'manure' on the phone to me," and canned him on the spot.

The Countess was a good customer. She ordered cut flowers by the pail, not the bunch, and if she liked a certain color in the roses, she'd buy six dozen twice a week. We'd come to an anteroom of her mansion to make our deliveries. We'd ring the bell, announce ourselves on a microphone, and wait for the buzzer to unlock the door. Then we'd come in with our flowers, set them in the empty room, and retreat outside. There we'd wait for a few minutes until the buzzer sounded again. Then we'd go back inside and collect our payment, which had now replaced the flowers on the floor (we never saw the person who did the replacing), along with a small bottle of perfume. The Countess had made a fortune in the perfume business and always tipped us with a sampling of her product.

One fall day twenty years ago, the Countess telephoned our place to announce her plan to create a giant culinary herb garden the following spring. Therefore, she wanted sixty plants of each of twelve different varieties of herbs commonly used in cooking, for delivery in May.

My father's specialties were asters, snapdragons, chrysanthemums, zinnias, and vegetables. He had never grown herbs commercially, though he knew how to, having always included a number of them in our kitchen garden and mixed in with our perennial flowers. He used some herbs as companion plants—to help keep pests away from certain vegetables—but mainly he grew them for our kitchen.

My father did not want to disappoint the Countess. That winter in the greenhouses, he sowed not sixty but a hundred herbs in each of the twelve categories—to be sure he ended up with all he needed to fill her order. The plantings were particularly successful, so in the spring, when the herbs were ready for moving outdoors, he found himself with quite a surplus.

We delivered the big order to the Countess, picked up our perfume, and came back to the garden center. Then we put the extra herb seedlings, which had been moved into 4-inch pots, out with the rest of the plants. When they sold out—almost immediately—my father turned to me and said, "Sal, quick, learn about herbs."

Behind the Herb Boom

To day we grow nearly two hundred different varieties of herbs, and though the basic culinary herbs account for eighty percent of our volume, about one third of our customers also buy and grow herbs for uses outside the kitchen.

The diversification into nonculinary herbs is relatively new. Two decades ago the market was not so broad. In fact, after the Countess showed us the way, I decided to include many nonculinary herbs in the sixty varieties we grew for our first real offering to the public. The following spring only the familiar herbs moved, however. Customers would read a label on the pot and say, "Oh, costmary, isn't that great!" But they wouldn't buy it.

Our customers are mainly suburban dwellers and back then men and women alike were far more interested in their lawns and their flowers than they were in herbs. Herbs played a minor role in their backyard scheme of things—for decoration or variety in rock gardens and such.

In 1969 Simon and Garfunkel's hit song, "Scarborough

Fair," extolled the virtues of "parsley, sage, rosemary, and thyme" and I figured that was all we needed to launch our herb business on a big scale.

I had a brainstorm that I could sell a lot of herbs at the Great Danbury Fair, an annual event which takes place about an hour's drive from our garden center.

So we rented a stall at the fair grounds and spent ten days up there trying to sell the fifteen thousand plants I had grown and potted for the occasion.

Seven hundred thousand people walked by our booth during that period. We sold a total of four hundred plants.

Obviously I was premature in my marketing plans—not to mention a bit naïve in expecting state fairgoers to lug parsley around instead of cotton candy.

In any case, times changed. Less than ten years later, we opened a similar booth at a much smaller fair in New York and we couldn't keep up with the business.

I attribute the growth in popularity of herbs since our 1969 Danbury venture to two things:

1. the revival of interest in vegetable gardening and in good home cooking, and

2. the willingness to experiment with herbs for medicinal or cosmetic purposes, using recipes and remedies that are as old as the hills.

Anyone who grows vegetables inevitably includes herbs in the garden plan, for their insect-repellent properties and for their value as flavoring agents in cooking.

Home-grown herbs are always better than store-bought herbs for cooking, by the way. In the first place, only fresh parsley and

chives are readily available in the stores. No one can mass market any of the other herbs effectively while fresh—sprigs of
thyme don't travel well. If you have your own garden you can
harvest the herbs minutes before throwing them into the pot, at
least during the growing season.

Your own dried or frozen herbs also are likely to be better
for winter use than commercially grown herbs. That's because
most commercial growers of culinary herbs use chemical ferti-
lizers to stimulate leaf growth in the plants in order to get a bigger
harvest. Generally, however, herbs that are forced into excessive
growth are not as flavorful as those that grow at their normal rate
in an organic soil.

I see people returning to home remedies based on herbs out
of frustration or disappointment with the medical profession, just
as people have returned to home vegetable gardens out of dis-
enchantment with the bland supermarket fare of the food con-
glomerates.

I am no expert in herbal home remedies myself, by the way.
My mother used to whip up a batch of rue and olive oil as a kind
of Ben-Gay for aching muscles when I was a kid. She'd make
chamomile tea for stomach aches. And if any of us ever looked a
little peaked while we were growing up, she'd blame it on "worms"
and make us eat a clove of garlic.

That's the extent of my direct experience of healing by herbs.
But I get enough customers these days buying horehound to make
cough and cold remedies, or getting mugwort to soothe their diges-
tive tracts, to know this is a large and growing field.

Another reason herbs have become more popular in recent
years is that more people are using them in centerpieces, sachets,

potpourris, and for herbal wreaths at Christmas. These and similar herb-intensive decorative objects are really more a function of fashion than anything else. The home gardening and healing pursuits come out of the more basic drive toward self-reliance that almost certainly will be part of our culture for some time to come.

Fashion is fickle in herbs as in anything else. Right now there appears to be more than an ordinary amount of interest in lavenders and scented geraniums, and in natural dye sources such as bedstraw and yarrow, so I'm planning to expand our plantings in these categories. But I won't overreact as I did two years ago.

Two years ago, thanks largely to an article in *Organic Gardening* on certain magical properties of comfrey, we sold all one thousand of our pots of that herb in the month of May. I planned ahead and was ready with twenty-five hundred pots of it the next year. But that spring no one wrote anything about comfrey and I was stuck with the batch.

We incorporated some of it in the compost piles—nitrogen-rich comfrey is a great compost-builder—and just dumped the rest in a back lot. Now we have a field full of comfrey, not to my surprise. I know by now that sometimes the less attention you give these herbs, the better they do.

Stalking the Elusive
Pink Hyssop

THERE WERE TWO main obstacles to learning about herbs "quick," as my father had directed.

First, there was a lack of clear-cut, detailed cultural information on herbs. Enough books have been written on these fascinating plants to fill a greenhouse, but most of the literature is devoted to lore and usage. It's easy to find out which herbs are related to which Zodiac signs, or what the Greeks used to think about sage, or how a tussy-mussy (a small herb bouquet) is constructed. But it hasn't been very easy to get accurate advice on how to grow the herbs. Only through trial and error, and frequent consultations with fellow growers, did I gradually develop the methods for sowing, growing, and maintaining herbs that I use today.

The second big problem I faced was that many sources for the herbs, and particularly for herbs started from seed, were frequently unreliable. The large seed companies, such as Burpee's or Park, only carried the basic culinary herbs, so I had to deal with small outfits and amateur herb growers to find a lot of the other herbs we needed.

I did not always get what we needed. I can't count the times I paid for golden oregano seed that grew green instead of yellow. It took me four years to locate a source for a seed that produced a true dwarf basil—a small-leaf plant much favored in Italian cuisine as a major ingredient in *pesto*, mainly because the people with the recipes feel it is a stronger-flavored variety. People advertised dwarf basil and I would order it, but since all types of basil seeds look alike, the only way to find out what we really had was to grow it.

It took me seven years to locate hyssop seed that actually produced pink and white flowering hyssop instead of the common blue flowering kind. The flowers don't emerge on this plant until August, so each time I'd buy "pink hyssop" or "white hyssop" it took me almost an entire growing season to find out I got blue.

It really requires professional harvesting, storing, and packing techniques—not to mention honesty in labeling—to develop good herb seed. Once I placed a substantial order for a wide range of seed through a mail-order firm that had sent me an impressive catalog. I enclosed my check for $63. A couple of weeks later I received a package with a fraction of the seed I had ordered and a refund check for $59. Many small seed catalogs made impressive offerings, I found, but often could not deliver on them.

After I noticed sweet woodruff had become very popular a few years ago, I ordered ten dollar's worth of seed from a reputable company and it came in a package marked: Germination Rate—92%. That told me I'd have all the sweet woodruff I could possibly use for the next season. But when I got around to trying to grow it, I had problems. I used my normal sowing techniques but nothing came up. I tried freezing the seed which, by providing something like the experience of hibernation to the seed, sometimes prompts it into sprouting; but that didn't work either. I even tried cracking the shell and bathing it in sulfuric acid, but still nothing happened.

Finally I called up the company and said, "What's this about ninety-two percent germination rate on sweet woodruff? I get zero percent."

"But it's true, when we cut open a sampling of the seeds, ninety-two percent were green and alive. However, we forgot to mention on the package that it takes a year from sowing for sweet woodruff to actually sprout."

Many seeds of herbs, I discovered, simply don't germinate unless they are sown soon after they are harvested. Sweet cicely and angelica are two that must be sown within two or three weeks after harvest or the seed fails to sprout in quantities worth the labor.

I used to think bay seed just naturally had a low germination rate but then I found that it too fared poorly "on the shelf." I would sow seven thousand bay seeds, acquired through a seed house in this country, and obtain less than seven hundred healthy plants. Then I began to get freshly harvested seed directly from Greece. When I sowed this seed, my germination rate for bay went from 10 to 80 percent.

How's Your Latin?

A LOT OF PEOPLE have been confused by the idea of herbs because they don't know exactly what they are. Others have been put off by the diverse nomenclature in the field.

The truth is, herbs cover a wide range of botanical families, so there is no precise way to define them scientifically.

Sometimes it's hard to say where weeds leave off and herbs begin, for instance. If you're a lawn fanatic, dandelions and purslane are weeds. If you're a salad lover, especially an Italian one, they're herbs.

I can't ship tansy plants into some cattle-growing states because it is outlawed. It's not regarded as a useful herb out there, but as a danger to livestock who have fed off it—eaten in large quantities, it induces abortion in pregnant cattle.

If you live in Connecticut, St. John's Wort is an herb that grows at a normal pace and comes in handy for treating nervous disorders. If you live in California, St. John's Wort is a weed that spreads so fast, it gives you a nervous disorder.

Keeping this theory of herbal relativity in mind, we can say that, basically, herbs are any soft-stemmed plants grown for their fragrance or flavor, or for their value to health and beauty.

They're not woody, like a shrub or tree is, and they're not exactly food crops, though some of them, such as onions, are as much food as flavor. And they're not spices, which come from the roots, bark, and fruit of tropical trees.

For the home gardener, the main thing that distinguishes herbs from flowers and vegetables is that most herbs are planted in units of ones and twos and threes, whereas most vegetables are planted in rows, and most flowers are planted in masses. It is probably this characteristic more than any other that encourages people to take their herb growing so personally. A row of lettuce is a row of lettuce. But a specimen bay plant is a pal.

There's a kind of language barrier in the field of herbs that has to be vaulted before people can appreciate the plants for what they are.

It takes patience to learn to differentiate between wild marjoram and sweet marjoram, say, or orange mint and peppermint, or French tarragon and its much-maligned impostor, Russian tarragon.

And it takes forbearance to tolerate yet another pun on the word "thyme," or to be told that the plant you're trying to buy is not dill but *Anethum graveolens*. Latin terms for plants are indispensable to advanced gardeners as a means of firmly identifying a plant from among dozens of similar varieties. But to the novice an excessive use of Latin smacks of snobbism.

I, myself, still have trouble with the terms used. Last year we got a wonderful order for one thousand plants for the new herb gardens being planned at the Cloisters in New York City. But all the plants were ordered by their true botanical names in Latin, and it took me half a day to translate them.

In any case, don't worry about what you call the different herbs. The word herb itself is rife with disputation. A friend of mine once gave a talk to a chapter of the Herb Society of America, a knowledgeable audience on this subject if there ever was one. But she conducted a poll and discovered even at these heights there was divided opinion on how to pronounce the word. Half of them pronounce it *herb*—with the "h"—she found, and the other half say *erb*.

Herbs Really Are for Everyone

HERBS ARE SO EASY to grow, if you do it right, and so universal in their appeal and utility, that I believe there is room for an herb garden in almost everyone's life.

That's the spirit in which this book has been conceived. The approach presented here is a broad one. It is designed to permit people to enjoy herb gardening according to their own tastes and needs, and the particular time and space available to them.

First, we will present that hard-to-find, nuts-and-bolts cultural information I mentioned earlier, in terms of a basic culinary herb garden. This will give readers a firm grasp on methods for growing those cooking herbs that are the most popular.

Then we will present fifteen herbs in detail, and by becoming familiar with each of them you will learn the growing techniques that work for virtually all the herbs.

In other words, once you have figured out how to successfully grow parsley, which is a biennial, for use in your salads and sauces, then you automatically know how to grow caraway, also a biennial, for your rye-bread-baking projects. And if you understand how to propagate sage or rosemary, then you can use the same techniques on lavender, a similar single-stem perennial.

Next, we will offer plans for all the other types of herb gardens of broad interest, so as to acquaint you with the wide range of growth patterns among herbs, and possibly to inspire you to venture beyond the ordinary kitchen herbs. All these plans will be presented in an eight-foot by eight-foot scheme, to provide a common standard that all readers can consult in developing gardens in their own special sites. We use the eight-by-eight size for convenience, as standard railroad ties come in that size and make excellent material for blocking in the garden area.

There is no law saying herb gardens have to be laid out in a formal pattern, and so long as the right cultural conditions are provided, the plants themselves wouldn't care if the garden looked like it had been built by a blind man on a jag. Generally, formal gardens laid out in geometric patterns take more care than the rough and ready variety. But don't automatically reject the idea of a formal garden, or link it with the leisure class or the artsy-craftsy. Underlying most formal garden plans is the desire to create, using semicircles and pathways and such, as much perimeter as possible, not for esthetic effect but in order to be able to tend and harvest the herbs conveniently.

We will also explore a number of functional and offbeat applications of herb gardening. Herbs can be used to cope with problem borders or shady spots in the yard, and many of them also can be adapted quite successfully for windowbox or container gardening. Herbs may be planted with stamp collector's zeal and satisfaction because in many categories, such as thyme or mint, they exist in dozens of varieties.

I guess it is the universality in herbs that makes me think no one should be without a garden made up of some of them. It is easier to be more successful, more quickly, with herbs than it is with flowers or vegetables because herbs don't require as much space, as rich a soil, or as much care, and in some cases, they don't even need as much sun.

Certainly there are herbs to suit everyone's taste and style of living.

If you're a party-giver, you can grow lemon verbena for your martinis, mint for juleps, and sweet woodruff for your May wine.

If you're a salad lover, you can devote your growing space entirely to tangy greens like sorrel and roquette.

If you're a lover, you can cultivate southernwood and valerian for your passion potions and aphrodisiacs—you'll at least have the power of suggestion going for you.

You can grow herbs simply for the esthetic value of their diverse foliage, or the contrasting or complementary color schemes available, especially in grays and greens.

If you grow flowers, you can grow some herbs, such as rosemary and sage, both for their uses in the kitchen and their attractive blooms. (See the Appendix for suggested culinary uses of the fifteen basic herbs.)

Nowadays I have many male customers coming in for the culinary herbs. In earlier times the herb garden was an important part of a woman's household tasks, but today men are in the kitchen, too.

So herbs are not for women only, nor for people in any particular age bracket. If anything, the return-to-nature movement seems to have brought more of the old people back into herbs.

Certainly my godmother, Antoinette, who is the Italian Euell Gibbons, has been vindicated. Years ago on her regular visits to Connecticut, she would make us salads that at the time we thought consisted of weeds. Now we know the ingredients were herbs, gathered by her in the wild, on the meadows and golf courses she passed on the drive up from New Jersey.

Young people are taking up herbs, too. One summer I had a couple of teenaged boys working for me who got so involved in the job that they started trying to grow varieties of their own. I was pleased that they took a shine to horticultural pursuits and spent so much time in ardent private conversations on the subject. I was pleased, that is, until I finally examined their growing projects up close and realized they had a small marijuana farm growing in the corner of one of the greenhouses.

Four Facts of Herb Life

BEFORE WE CONSIDER the first herb garden, let's analyze the general conditions that determine how individual herbs grow. An herb's *life cycle, climate, growth pattern,* and *means of propagation* dictate what you can and can't do in the garden for all the herbs. Becoming familiar with these key factors is really more important, at this point, than knowing which names belong to which herbs.

Life Cycle

Herbs live according to one of three distinctly different timetables: annual, perennial, or biennial.

An *annual* is any plant which can be sown from seed and will mature to harvest stage within one growing season. Left outside, both plant and root structure will be killed by frost.

Many of the culinary herbs are annuals—basil, chervil, coriander, dill, summer savory.

A *perennial* is a plant that comes back every spring. The plant itself may be killed by frost, but the root structure is hardy and, after hibernating for the winter, it sends up new shoots at the crack of spring.

Mints, marjoram, tarragon, sage, and oregano are all perennials.

A *biennial* is a plant that takes two years to mature. Its root structure survives the first winter it spends outdoors, but when the plant quickly goes to seed in the second growing season, it is usually finished.

Parsley is the most familiar of the relatively few biennial herbs.

Climate

Life cycle and climate obviously are interrelated.

Since all annuals are killed by frost, they must all be tender. But some are more tender than others. A forty-degree night with a wind will kill a basil plant but not affect the borage plant right next to it. Both are annuals, but basil is very tender and borage is not.

Most perennials are hardy but some don't survive the winter the way they're supposed to because their root structures die in severe cold weather. Bay and rosemary are good examples of perennial herbs that must be treated as annuals up North. One of my customers manages to keep her rosemary alive through the winter only because the plant is in front of the vent for her clothes dryer, and this particular woman does a lot of laundry.

The other side of the coin is that some perennials don't do well in the *absence* of cold winter. Roses and perennial spring bulbs don't do well down south because the weather doesn't permit them to hibernate and recoup their energies. They are also more susceptible to insects down there.

Sunlight is important to all herbs in varying degrees. Some will tolerate partial shade, but few will really do well in total shade for long. Most herbs achieve their best growth in full sun. It is the long hours of sunlight that force the herbs to produce the oils that give them their unique aroma or flavor in the first place.

Rate and Pattern of Growth

Knowing the size, shape, and spreading pattern of each herb is indispensable to a successful garden plan. Think of herb gardening as landscape architecture practiced on a small scale. Each herb must be located to complement its neighbor and not get in the other's way.

Perennials must be given more room from the start since they are permanent residents which will get bigger every year.

Some perennials grow on a single stem, others via an underground network of roots and new shoots. It is the latter, or spreading perennials, that must be watched carefully, and periodically dug up and reduced to keep them within bounds. A single mint plant left untended in good growing conditions will spread five feet in every direction within three years.

The individual herb's potential for growing tall or wide,

above ground, also must be considered. Herbs such as angelica, lovage, or Jerusalem artichoke, which reach six feet in height, should be put at the back of the garden so they don't shade the other plants or block your view of them.

Other herbs may be kept in place by cutting back. Rosemary will grow four feet wide if you let it.

Some herbs, such as parsley or chive, grow effectively in rows, and others may be trained into low hedges, such as teucrium and santolina.

Certain herbs have almost freakish rates of growth. Borage will crowd out its neighbors in a matter of weeks in early spring if you've planted things too close together. Bee balm and lemon verbena start slowly in spring but bush out dramatically in summer if left untended.

Means of Propagation

The four best ways to coax new herbs into life are from seed sown by the gardener, from cuttings of stems or branches, from divisions of root systems, or from seed sown by the plant itself.

All annuals are started from seed, and it is relatively easy to do so. These herbs may be sown directly into the designated area in the garden, or planted as seedlings after having been started from seed in planting pots or trays indoors. This indirect sowing method is useful in northern climates to get a jump on the season.

Some perennials may also be started from seed, but it is easier, with single-stem perennials, to take cuttings off an exist-

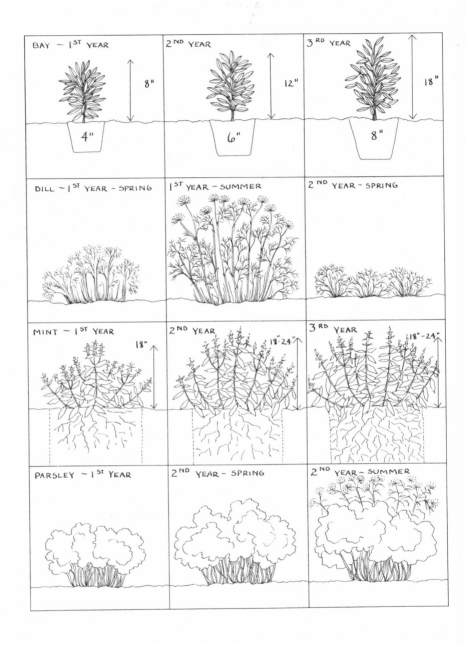

BAY ~ 1ST YEAR   8"   4"

2ND YEAR   12"   6"

3RD YEAR   18"   8"

DILL ~ 1ST YEAR - SPRING

1ST YEAR - SUMMER

2ND YEAR - SPRING

MINT ~ 1ST YEAR   18"

2ND YEAR   18"-24"

3RD YEAR   18"-24"

PARSLEY ~ 1ST YEAR

2ND YEAR - SPRING

2ND YEAR ~ SUMMER

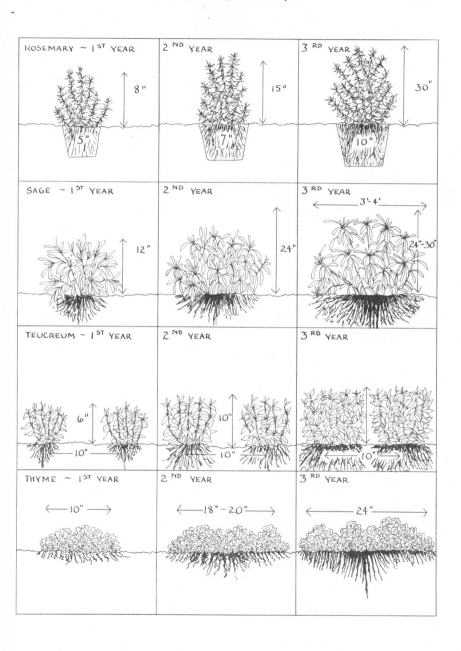

ing healthy plant and place the branch in a sand/perlite mixture. Properly watered and lighted, this shoot will send out new roots in a short while.

It is even easier to propagate spreading perennials like the mint family. By digging up the root system of an established plant, one can divide the findings into as many new plants as needed.

Finally, there are the herbs which produce their own seed in the course of the growing season and, with a little luck, resow themselves in and around the area of the original plant. Annuals such as dill, and perennials such as marjoram or sage, commonly produce these so-called volunteers, which make their appearance in the garden the next spring, and invariably prompt at least one customer a year to run into our garden center declaring, "Sal, my dill's a perennial!"

PART II

Building the First Garden

IN THIS SECTION we'll concentrate on developing a basic herb garden consisting of fifteen common culinary herbs for growing in a sunny eight-by-eight area.

A small garden such as this is best to start with. It can be constructed in three hours, placed in any sunny spot in the yard, and easily expanded in subsequent years if desired.

The trouble with starting too big, or with too elaborate a design in mind, is that you may not get the project off the ground, or you'll do it in a slipshod fashion. Or you'll end up with an area that's really too large for your present interests, needs, or abilities. Herb gardening is supposed to be pleasurable and relatively carefree, not a burden, so set your sights small at the start.

I use the specific dimensions of eight feet by eight simply because it is convenient to create the raised bed I recommend by obtaining commercially available eight-foot-long railroad ties. You may desire or have on hand other strong barrier materials just as suitable for defining the raised bed area—concrete blocks or two-by-ten-inch lumber also work fine. These other materials may dictate different dimensions. In any case, so long as you wind up with about sixty to seventy-five square feet in a sunny location, you'll have plenty of room for the first garden.

The raised bed itself is important because almost all herbs need well-drained soil conditions to do well. This was brought home to me dramatically one year when I visited a six-acre commercial planting of tarragon in Ohio. The soil in the fields seemed almost bone dry, but when I dug up a couple of plants, I saw they had lush and complex root systems.

There are some secondary benefits of a raised bed, too. Such a garden is often esthetically more pleasing, for it stands apart from its surroundings dramatically and creates a kind of centerpiece effect in the yard. The raised bed is easier to keep under control for there is little chance of the herbs wandering beyond the garden barriers, or of unwanted grass and weeds spreading into the garden from the edges. Finally, it is easier to tend and cultivate the raised bed because you don't have to bend as far to reach it. If you like, you can sit on the barrier material to do your harvesting.

Unless your soil is extremely porous and gravelly, it may well hold the moisture from rainfall or watering too long to do your herbs good. Certainly the main cause of herb loss in the home garden among my own customers here in Connecticut has been poorly drained soil. With a raised bed of proper soil tilth and consistency, this problem is avoided.

Railroad ties cost $8 to $10 apiece new, but you can get used ones cheaper, and you can also scavenge for them along railroad lines where track beds are being modernized. This is a dirty job and it requires a truck or station wagon, but if you're strong and economy-minded it's just the ticket. Telephone poles are similarly re-placed at intervals and you can cart them away in manageable lengths if you know where and when the crews are doing the job.

In shopping for new railroad ties, beware of buying ones treated with creosote, a wood preservative that is deadly to vege-tative life. A friend of mine in the garden business once stained all the wood benches in one of his greenhouses with the stuff and the fumes killed $5,000 worth of his house plants.

So buy your railroad ties *untreated* and, if you want to coat them to prolong their usefulness, use Cuprinol, a product that I've found does not impair plant growth. Or get the old railroad ties. The creosote remaining on them will not be strong enough to hurt your herbs. If you want to play extra safe, paint the ties with varnish.

Creating the right soil mix in the raised bed—soil, sand, and peat moss in equal amounts, plus some perlite—is another expense, but it's an essential investment for most gardeners, too. To fill an eight-by-eight area to a depth of six to eight inches would cost about $25 if you had to buy all the ingredients, which are:

• Topsoil ($5 for 6 cubic feet)—as the basic food source for the herbs.

• Sand ($4 for 6 cubic feet)—to allow the entire soil mix to drain rapidly.

• Peat moss ($10 for 6 cubic feet)—to condition the mix, by loosening the soil and blending with it. (You could use sphag-num moss instead of peat moss but it is much more expensive and its coarser character has no particular value in herb growing.)

• Perlite ($6 for 3 cubic feet), which is crushed volcanic matter, or pumice—to lighten the soil. (You might use vermiculite instead of perlite but this corklike matter derived from mica tends to retain moisture, which is not so good for most herbs, so I definitely favor the perlite.)

You should buy these materials if your soil is poor or claylike or if you're constructing the garden on top of an existing lawn area. In the latter case, you should also be sure to break up the sod with a grub ax or spade and turn it grass-side down before filling in the area with the topsoil, sand, peat moss, and perlite. Once these ingredients have been thoroughly blended with a spade fork, the soil should be tested for its degree of acidity or alkalinity. Generally, most herbs do best in very slightly acid soil with a 5.5 to 6.5 pH reading. Dill, basil, and parsley benefit in a slightly sweeter soil but it's not essential to add lime in those spots to get a decent crop. Your Cooperative Extension Service (see Appendix) will analyze a sample of your soil for a small fee or at no charge.

The fifteen herbs I recommend for the first garden all have immediate practical value in the kitchen. Also, taken together, growing them happens to involve virtually every trick or technique for growing practically all the herbs. They are:

chives
marjoram
thyme

basil
coriander
chervil

parsley
dill
summer savory

mint
oregano
tarragon

sage
rosemary
bay

The easiest way to get this first garden going is to buy all fifteen herbs as established plants and simply transplant them to your prepared soil bed. I recommend doing this if you can find a professional local supplier of fresh herbs. The plants are usually available in 3- or 4-inch pots and sell for $1 to $2.50 apiece.

The transplanting may be done as early as one month prior to your spring frost date for the hardy plants among these herbs:

chives
marjoram
thyme

parsley

mint
oregano

tarragon

sage

The tender herbs should not be placed out until all danger of frost is past. These are:

coriander

chervil

dill

summer savory

rosemary and bay (tender perennials)

And wait yet another two weeks to plant the ultra-sensitive:

basil

You may locate the herbs within the garden area any way you like, within reason. The plan on page 105 suggests one possible arrangement. It is not completely arbitrary, for "the four facts of herbal life" influenced the design, specifically as follows:

All the spreading perennials—marjoram, mint, oregano and tarragon—have been given relatively more space in which to grow than the other herbs.

The shorter herbs—thyme, marjoram, and parsley—have been placed in the front or on the edge of the garden and the tallest-growing herbs—dill, tarragon, and coriander—are in the back.

Two additional features are worthy of note though not apparent in the plan itself—because they're underground.

The mint, most rampant grower of the spreading perennials, should be literally boxed in below soil to prevent its growing beyond its bounds in future years by sinking Masonite boards or some similar durable material to a depth of 8 to 10 inches to create a 15-inch square confined growing area. If you can find inexpensive chimney casing units, they'll work even better.

The bay and rosemary are in clay pots buried at soil level. That's because, as tender perennials, eventually they will require protection from the cold, at least wherever winter temperatures fall below 20° F. Keeping these two herbs in pots makes them much more easily removed to a sunny window indoors in the late fall. This method also keeps root systems from spreading so much. If you planted your bay and rosemary without pots, the plants would develop deep tap roots that would have to be severed in order to pot them up in the fall and would have filled out so much otherwise that you'd need unmanageably large pots to handle them.

The one drawback in keeping bay and rosemary in pots in the garden is that the plants will tend to dry out more quickly, so they must be watched carefully and watered more often during droughts.

Starting from Scratch

THE EASIEST WAY to get started in herb gardening is to buy all the herb plants you need.

Unfortunately, good suppliers of fresh herb plants are few and far between. Most garden centers that sell vegetable transplants in the spring do offer chives, parsley, and basil as plants, but often they won't have any of the other herbs. Most growers can't be bothered with herbs, or don't really know how to go about raising more than a few types, or simply don't want to get involved in answering questions from customers about a subject they themselves don't know much about.

Unless you happen to live within driving range of a place like ours then, you're going to have to start your own plants.

Buying the fresh plants by mail-order would be an alternative—and we are in that business, too. The rub here is the postal system. If an herb plant gets delayed in transit beyond four days —and even First Class deliveries are taking that long presently—its health and vigor are jeopardized, and it may not even survive.

Starting from scratch, without the benefit of established

plants, or without some local herb expert to coach you through the first season, does have one big advantage, as I've mentioned already. Hard and complex as it may seem at times, this approach will make you thoroughly familiar with the techniques for knowing and growing all the herbs, in a way that starting from established plants would not.

I also think that if you focus on learning to grow the fifteen basic cooking herbs, you'll emerge a much better all-around herb gardener than if you tried to absorb cultural information about hundreds of herbs in mind-boggling alphabetical order (as it is frequently presented).

We'll discuss the basic herbs in five sets of three. Each threesome happens to involve a different technique or somewhat different conditions for successful growing. Remember, once you've learned to grow these fifteen herbs, you'll know how to grow most other herbs with just a minimum of additional information. So it's worth taking the time and trouble to do those fifteen right.

The indoor sowing activities to be described commence about three months before the average date of the last frost in the spring in your neck of the woods. You can determine this date for your locale by asking the Cooperative Extension Service (listed in local phone books) or a knowledgeable local source such as your garden center. In my area of Connecticut, May 15 has been statistically determined to be the last day we're likely to get a frost. So in this area February 15 would be the time to sow the first group of herbs indoors.

A certain amount of indoor sowing is a necessity up north. If we waited until the soil was warm enough to sow the seed directly outdoors, in many cases no crop of any significance would develop before the end of our short growing season.

Indoor sowing also makes sense simply because so many of the herb seeds are tiny. Outdoors they can be crushed or kicked or washed away. Indoors they can be nurtured into life under proper supervision.

It's a good idea to stick to the timing suggested for sowing the various seeds indoors. The slow-growing herbs need all the time stipulated in order to develop properly. And the ones that grow quickly get leggy if kept inside beyond their time. Keep them all on schedule (See Appendix for precise planting dates), and you'll have healthy plants to put into the garden when the time comes.

What You'll Need to Start Herbs from Seed Indoors

INDOOR SOWING of herbs in small quantities doesn't take much room at all, but there are certain materials, devices, methods, and conditions that help insure success. Let me describe them here briefly before getting into the sowing and growing of the specific herb groups.

Southern Exposure. The best location in the home for developing herb seedlings is a window with a sunny southern exposure—one that is exposed to sunlight all day long in the winter. If you can set your pots and trays on the windowsill or a table at this location, you should be able to develop the herbs properly. A shelf or table area that is 3 feet long and 6 to 9 inches wide, positioned directly in this window, will give you all the space you need.

If your best window is oriented somewhat southwest or southeast, you won't get as much of the sunlight available and your seedlings will tend to lean in the direction of the missing sun. That simply means you'll have to rotate the plants every three or four days to keep them growing reasonably erect.

Calculate the amount of sunlight your best window gets before you begin the sowing, say in mid-February. If the sun shines into that window for seven to eight hours, you're sitting pretty. You could get away with a little less light before germination, but after the seeds have sprouted the eight-hour exposure is essential. Without it the plants would grow weak and spindly very quickly.

If your most convenient window location doesn't attract the minimum sunlight required, you can make up for it by bringing in fluorescent lights. For every hour of the required natural sunlight your site misses, expose the plants to two hours of fluorescent light. For example, if your window receives only six hours of sun, add four hours of fluorescent light, which in total is the equivalent of about eight hours of natural sunlight.

Temperature. The best temperature for developing good herb plants indoors is 70° before germination and 60 to 65° after germination. The energy crisis has lowered average household temperatures somewhat in recent years and more homes now have the correct range for herbs.

A higher temperature can be created if necessary by covering the pots with a thin sheet of clear polyethylene plastic tacked to a simple frame. This will increase the temperature 5 to 10 degrees, help retain moisture greenhouse-style, and so stimulate much better germination. Be sure to remove the poly once sprouting occurs.

Seed. Herb seed is not readily available, at least not in variety, on the standard flower and vegetable seed racks. You'll have to order most of it through a reputable seed house. (See Appendix for a listing of recommended sources.) Order the seed in December or early January so it arrives in time. One packet of each will be more than enough for your first garden. About 50 to 100 seeds come to the packet for most varieties. This varies with each supplier, and also from year to year within the same seed house. In recent years the trend has been to include fewer and fewer seeds. Anyway, you'll need only about a fourth of the seed for the first year. The rest is insurance, against an extremely low germination rate, or an accident such as the cat knocking over the whole project.

Planting Mix. The soil/sand/peat moss/perlite mixture described earlier for the outdoor soil bed is indispensable for indoor sowing. A bag of commercial potting soil should be your source of the soil part of the formula for convenience and also because, unlike your garden soil, it is already sterilized and completely free of stones and such. The stringier and more expensive sphagnum moss may be used in place of the peat moss but you'll have to break it up a bit with your fingers.

Don't underestimate the importance of starting with the right mix to sow the seeds in. I'm so convinced of its value that I've started bagging the blend in small quantities for my own customers. Please don't make the mistake, as many novice gardeners have done, of trying to start herb seed in any of the various commercial planting mixes or "herb seed kits" available, especially those containing vermiculite. These mixes are not really designed with herbs in mind. None of them will drain quickly enough for sowing some of the more delicate varieties. I spend half the month of March looking at customers' dead or dying seedlings that they have tried to grow in such mixes.

Cutting Mix. We recommend growing certain herbs, not from seed, but from cuttings—small branches snipped or snapped off from an existing plant. Placed in the proper rooting mixture, these cuttings eventually send out roots and become established as new plants. The best rooting medium for these cuttings consists of one part sand and one part perlite. You'll have these ingredients on hand already if you've acquired what you need for the ideal planting mix mentioned above. We eliminate the soil and peat moss from the cutting mix to improve drainage to the maximum, for cuttings are extremely susceptible to many fungus problems.

Play Sand. A bag of this fine clean sand (readily available in hardware stores or toy stores) will be more than enough for your needs, but it's well worth getting. The trick is to sprinkle a thin layer of the play sand over the herb seed after you have made your sowing. The sand is heavy enough to keep the tiny, buoyant seeds in their place during the germination period. And it is fine enough to drain quickly, so that after sprouting the herb seedlings will not have too much moisture around the base of their stems, and so will not be likely to perish from dampening-off, a fungus-produced rotting of the tender new shoot above the soil line, which is the No. 1 problem immediately after germination. Basil and sage are particularly susceptible to dampening-off.

Planting Pots. If you have any gardening experience at all, you probably have various containers handy already, or you can improvise with confidence. If you're a rank beginner, you should acquire a half-dozen 3- to 4-inch diameter clay pots (plastic pots are not as desirable because they're not as porous and so may retain moisture too long), a half-dozen peat pots of about the same size, and several 5-by-7-inch "market packs"—the trays that vegetable seedlings come in at garden centers in the spring. That's all you'll need for the indoor sowing project.

When the time comes, fill the pots with your planting mix. Make sure the mix is level and slightly damp. If it is bone dry, sprinkle it thoroughly twenty-four hours before sowing. It should not be soggy wet when it's time to receive the seed.

A Container for the Containers. It's much easier to control the indoor sowing project if all your working pots and trays can be held in one larger leak-proof tray or box. This is not an abso-lute necessity, but it will make it easy for you later on to put all your young seedlings outside on the odd balmy early spring day. More important, it can be used effectively to prevent any of the herbs from standing in water, a condition which quickly promotes rotting in herb roots. The trick is to cover the bottom of your con-tainer with a layer of pebbles, and then set your planting pots and market packs on top of the pebbles. That way, when you do irri-gate, any excess water will drain through the bottom of the pots and out of contact with the root systems—which will have devel-oped all the way down to the bottom of the pots toward the end of their time indoors.

Mister. For use *before* germination. This could be a con-verted Windex bottle or any other spray-type container in which certain household products have been sold. Once it has been thoroughly washed and rinsed, it can be filled with lukewarm water and used for keeping the planting mix moist during the ger-mination period, without disrupting the soil or dislodging the tiny seeds, as might happen if you watered with a conventional water-ing can or, God forbid, submitted your pots and trays to a cascade under the kitchen faucet. Many growers submerge the seeded pots or trays in water for several minutes and allow the medium to absorb the water from the bottom. This is an excellent procedure but it's probably too time-consuming for most people—and also too messy for most homes.

Watering Can. For use *after* germination. Any manageably small indoor-type watering can will do.

Fertilizer. The herb seedlings will require one small dose of fertilizer at a certain stage in their development. I recommend using a natural or organic type fertilizer such as fish emulsion or liquid seaweed. This is what we use in our greenhouses and it works fine. The small amount you'll need won't cost much. You can buy it at most garden centers. Or you can irrigate with skim milk instead of water. I've used skim milk successfully on herb seedlings in their early stages. It really promotes healthy growth —unless your cat gets into it.

Insect Repellent. Herbs are not bug-attractive and in fact they are frequently used in vegetable patches by organic gardeners because they tend to keep bugs away. Even in greenhouses, where insects can be a real problem, our herbs stay relatively clean. Your house plants are much more likely to harbor insects than your herb plants. If you have a lot of house plants, watch more carefully for bugs in your herbs.

For all that, if you should spot bugs, a good way to get rid of them fast is to mix up a batch of something known in my family as Nana's Bug Juice. Put a couple of cloves of garlic and some cayenne pepper in a half cup of water or cider vinegar and pour into a blender. Mix the ingredients thoroughly, then pour them through a piece of cheesecloth or some other filtering device so that you end up with a clear solution. Pour this into your mister and then spray the affected plants.

This spray will work at least as well as any chemical spray and won't coat your plants with anything poisonous or unpalatable. These herbs are food crops, of course, and people are always plucking their leaves to eat them. With this in mind you're more likely to take a strictly nonchemical approach, as I do, to growing herbs. You'll also want to eschew the soap-and-water treatment some people use on their house plants.

Cooling-Off Place. This is required to expose the herb plants to cooler outdoor temperatures before finally setting them out in the garden. A cold frame would be ideal but an unheated room or screened-in porch with good light is almost as effective. If you don't have either, then set the plants outside for a few hours on warm days when the time comes, only be sure to protect them from the harsh winds that are so common in early spring. Something made of plastic that surrounds the plants on three sides will prevent the wind from setting the herbs back.

Pad and Pencil. It's a good idea to maintain at least an informal journal of your herb-growing activities. If you note down when you sowed each herb, when sprouts first appeared, etc., you'll perform the later steps in handling each herb at the right time and with more confidence generally, and you'll be much better prepared when next year rolls around.

Cluster Sowing Indoors

Group 1: CHIVES

MARJORAM

THYME

NOW LET'S DESCRIBE the ways to get the basic culinary herbs into your first garden from scratch.

The way to start the first group of chives, marjoram, and thyme indoors is by cluster sowing. This means evenly sprinkling the seed across the planting surface of a 4-inch pot, then covering it with play sand and misting daily until germination.

Use clay pots rather than peat pots for this group. The plants will be in the pots for a longer period of time. Also chives and marjoram have heavy root systems that benefit from confinement. They wouldn't be as happy in a biodegradable pot.

Figure on using 10 to 20 seeds of marjoram and thyme per pot, but be more generous with the chives—say 15 to 25 seeds— as chives develop best in clumps.

The chive seed will be easy to handle because it's flat and

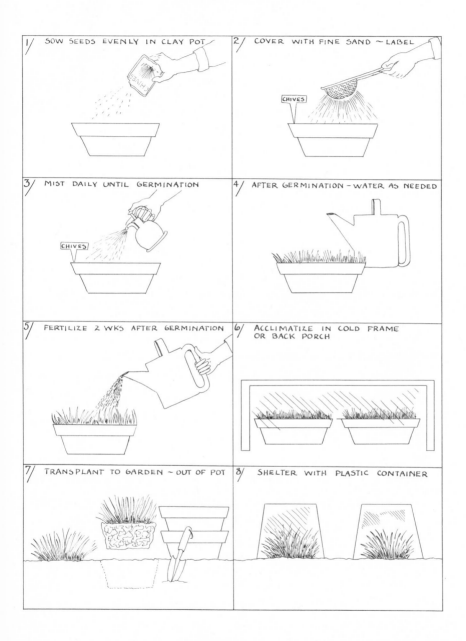

1/ SOW SEEDS EVENLY IN CLAY POT

2/ COVER WITH FINE SAND ~ LABEL

CHIVES

3/ MIST DAILY UNTIL GERMINATION

CHIVES

4/ AFTER GERMINATION – WATER AS NEEDED

5/ FERTILIZE 2 WKS AFTER GERMINATION

6/ ACCLIMATIZE IN COLD FRAME OR BACK PORCH

7/ TRANSPLANT TO GARDEN ~ OUT OF POT

8/ SHELTER WITH PLASTIC CONTAINER

at least five times bigger than the marjoram or thyme seed. You can shake it out of the seed package with good control. Take an extra minute to sow the smaller seeds from between your finger-tips, though. Make sure the thyme and marjoram seeds fall where you want them to grow and they won't choke each other out later on.

Cluster sowing permits all three herbs to grow in a fairly thick stand and so creates a stronger unit for moving into the garden, and gives you much more productivity in the first year.

You couldn't sow most vegetables this way, but these herb plants don't have the high nutritional needs that would make them compete with each other, and eventually suffer, in such limited space. The grouping of chive, marjoram, and thyme plants that should emerge in each 4-inch pot will all do fine.

You could sow only two or three seeds, rather than a cluster of them, in each pot, but then it would take so much longer for these perennials to spread enough to give you plenty to pick from for the kitchen. With these particular herbs, you can get there faster by cluster sowing.

Thyme and marjoram take four to five days to germinate, chives about seven days.

During this pre-germination period, the pots should be kept in natural light but preferably not in full direct sunlight. If there's a chance they'll sprout in full sun when you're out of the house for a couple of days, cover the seedbed with a piece of cheesecloth or burlap. That will keep the seedlings from wither-ing away before you get back.

Mist the pots every morning until shoots appear, to keep the soil moist—but without creating flood conditions.

After germination, start using the watering can, but do so

carefully—irrigating only when the soil surface is dry to the touch, only in the mornings, and only at the base of the plants, keeping water off the stems and leaves of the seedlings as best you can.

Fertilize with liquid fish emulsion or skim milk about two weeks after germination. Fill a watering can and dissolve the fertilizer in the water according to the proportions given on the label. One shot of the extra food—about three tablespoons per pot of the spiked water—is all the seedlings will need to get firmly established. If you water them with this solution, you'll give the plants the correct amount of food. If you're going to use skim milk instead of fertilizer, just "water" with skim milk.

In another month, the herbs will be ready to go into the garden. At this time the chives should be about six inches high and the lower-growing thyme and marjoram about four inches high. If they get much taller than this, and it is still too soon to safely put them out in the garden, simply cut them back to two inches high and eat the clippings. The cutting back makes the plants stronger.

As hardy perennials, chives, marjoram, and thyme are resistant to frost, and that's why they can go into the garden a month *before* the last date of frost in the spring.

However, since these plants have never had the experience of being outdoors, it would be a good idea to introduce them to conditions in that world gradually during the last week before transplanting them. This can be done by setting them out in your cooling-off place. Then, when the time comes to knock the soil ball out of each pot and plant it intact in the garden, the herbs will accept the transfer without a complaint.

If, after they have been set out, there is unusually cold

weather, with sub-freezing temperatures predicted, the herbs would be happier under some temporary protection. Half-gallon clear plastic ice-cream containers are easy to come by and are well-suited for this purpose. Put a stone on top to prevent the wind blowing the protection away.

Spot Sowing Indoors

Group 2: BASIL

CHERVIL

CORIANDER

UNLIKE THE PRECEDING HERBS, basil, chervil, and
coriander are all *tender*. They can't be put out in the garden until
after all danger of frost is past. Therefore, these should be started
from seed indoors about a month after you've started the chives,
marjoram, and thyme. Then they won't spend too much time
waiting.

This group of herbs may be started the same way you started
chives, marjoram, and thyme, with one big difference. Instead of
sprinkling a dozen seeds as you did for each perennial, sow *only
3 to 4 seeds per pot* for the basil, chervil and coriander. Then,
when the new seedlings are about one to two inches high, pluck
out all but the healthiest from each pot. That's the one plant you'll
nurture for the garden.

Use peat pots for this group if possible. Since we're starting

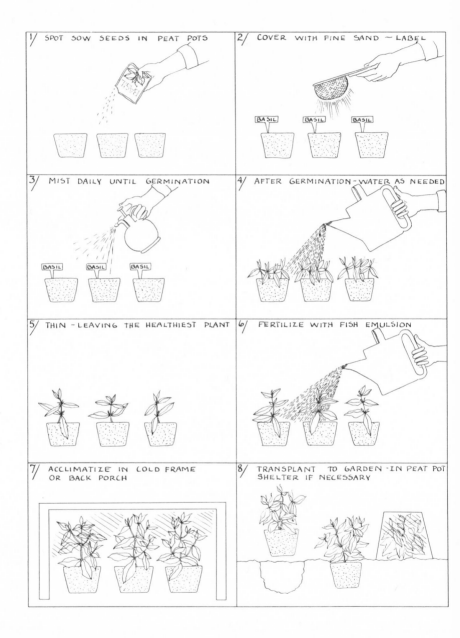

them later you don't have to worry about the pot disintegrating before the plants are ready to go in the garden. Also, because their root systems are more delicate than those of most herbs, they can be protected from disturbance simply by planting them, pot and all. This couldn't be done if you had used a clay or plastic pot.

Just to be sure there's no confusion, here's the spot sowing method a step at a time:

Fill 4-inch pots with your planting mix and make sure the mix is level and reasonably moist. Sow 3 to 4 seeds of each herb in its own pot. Label the pots to prevent mixups later.

Cover the seed with fine sand, place the pots in a well-lighted place and mist every day until sprouts appear, which should be in about one week.

After germination, keep providing good light and water carefully as needed.

In three to four weeks, when the seedlings are approximately two inches high, thin to one herb per pot. Save the healthiest— the seedling with the greenest color and thickest stem. When you weed out the rejects, protect the seedling to remain by gently pressing down on the soil around it with two fingers.

Fertilize lightly with liquid fish emulsion or skim milk in about a week. Continue watering as needed. In another three weeks the basil and chervil should stand four to six inches high and the coriander six to eight inches high.

They are now just about ready for setting out into the garden. First, though, acclimatize them to outdoor conditions for a few days in your cooling-off place, especially the basil, the most tender of the herbs. Even with temperatures up in the fifties, a 15 to 20 mph wind could hurt it. To be on the safe side, don't put it out into the garden until about two weeks after your spring frost date.

Plant the herbs where you want them in your garden, peat pot and all. Bury the pot rims below soil too, so they don't act like a wick and drain the moisture out of the soil. Or, simply break the rims off.

Use those ice cream containers to protect the young plants after this, should the weather turn cold.

Cluster Sowing Outdoors

Group 3: PARSLEY

SUMMER SAVORY

DILL

THIS GROUP MAY BE sown directly outdoors because the herbs will develop fast enough after sprouting to give you a good crop by the end of the summer. But wait until at least spring frost date to make these sowings.

Here's a trick for creating a planting site for each herb that will warm up the soil for quicker germination, protect each area from the elements before and after germination, and keep your sowing areas clearly marked—so you don't step on them by mistake in the early stages.

About two or three days *before* you plan to sow your seed, prepare and level the soil in the spots you've selected for each of the three herbs within your garden area. Cut up an empty half-gallon milk carton into three 3-inch-high temporary frames, one for each of the sowing areas. Then cover each frame with a patch

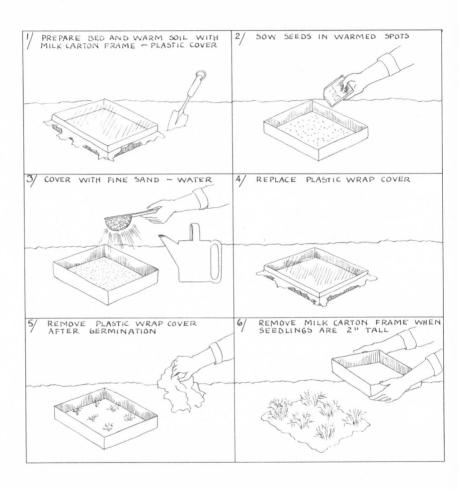

1/ PREPARE BED AND WARM SOIL WITH MILK CARTON FRAME ~ PLASTIC COVER

2/ SOW SEEDS IN WARMED SPOTS

3/ COVER WITH FINE SAND ~ WATER

4/ REPLACE PLASTIC WRAP COVER

5/ REMOVE PLASTIC WRAP COVER AFTER GERMINATION

6/ REMOVE MILK CARTON FRAME WHEN SEEDLINGS ARE 2" TALL

of clear plastic—you could even use plastic sandwich bags secured around each frame with rubber bands.

Sink the frames into the soil an inch—deep enough to make them secure—at the chosen sites.

The soil inside these three miniature greenhouses will warm up much faster than that in the rest of the garden. In a couple of days it'll be ready to receive your seeds.

On the day of sowing, remove the plastic, sprinkle about 10 to 20 seeds of each herb in each of the selected areas, then cover with fine sand. Water thoroughly before replacing the plastic cover.

During the germination period, the clear plastic tops will let the sunlight come through and keep the soil bed warm, but will prevent any hard spring rain from creating havoc.

Sprouts should appear in five days for the dill and summer savory, but not for two weeks for the more methodical parsley. Remove the plastic then and, after the plants are well established— say two inches high—remove the milk carton frame as well. Don't bother thinning unless you have an exceptionally thick stand from oversowing.

Test sowing of herb seed. Though it's not really necessary if you have fresh seed from a reputable supplier, you could test sow the parsley, summer savory, and dill indoors at the same time you're toiling over the earlier groups. Test sowing is definitely advisable if you're working with leftover seed from previous years. Fill a 5-by-7-inch container with your soil mix and make three shallow furrows. Sow 10 seeds of each herb per row. Then cover with fine sand and mist every day until germination. Now count. If you get 7 or 8 out of 10 seeds to germinate in each row, it means the seed is good. When the time comes for sowing out-doors, you can be confident you'll get good results. Anything below 50 percent germination means you're going to have to sow more seed, when the time comes, to get the thick stand of plants you'll want. If you only get 20 or 30 percent germination, I'd throw the package out and find a new supplier before your spring sowing date.

In any case, don't throw out the seedlings from your test sowing. Harvest them and use them in a salad.

Making Divisions of Spreading Perennials

Group 4: MINT
TARRAGON
OREGANO

T H E   B E S T   W A Y   T O start these three perennials in your garden, when you can't buy them, is to divide established plants from
somebody else's garden.

Actually, mint and oregano may also be started from seed,
but it is much easier to get them from a division, which amounts
to Instant Plant.

Mint takes at least a month to germinate and is a little tricky.
If you have the patience of a saint, you can do it from seed.

It's very hard to find the right seed for true oregano—I mean
the genuine, pizza-quality oregano as opposed to the bland pot
marjoram variety, or the "wild marjoram," that is often passed
off as the real thing. Actually, even if you had harvested your

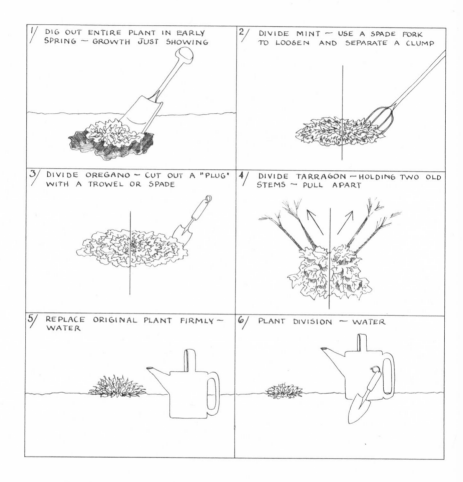

own seed from an oregano plant of proven tastiness, often something would be lost in the succeeding plant generation and it would not have the distinctive oregano flavor.

In my own garden, at least, this appears to be the fault of the bees, who commute indiscriminately between oregano blossoms in one part of the garden and pot marjoram blossoms in another. The resulting cross-pollination, I suspect, is what adulterates the oregano seed later on. Anyway, that's why when I want to start new oregano plants I always prefer to make divisions or cuttings from the bona fide plants.

As for true French tarragon, it does not produce seed, so there's nothing to sow with. Russian tarragon produces seed and that is what is offered in some herb seed catalogs. But it has such a bland flavor that it doesn't belong in the basic culinary garden.

The French tarragon, like oregano, may also be started from a cutting, according to a method I'll describe shortly for the last group of herbs. However, it's much easier to propagate the plant by division, and that's why I place it in this group.

The time to make divisions of perennial herbs is when they first begin to show life again in the new season—approximately four to six weeks before the spring frost date. At this time you can hack away at each plant without seriously hampering life and growth potential. These perennials which spread by meandering root systems underground actually benefit by periodic division, for the operation prevents them from choking on their own prolix growth pattern.

Thus, early spring is the time to launch a search for friends, relatives, neighbors, and, if necessary, total strangers—anyone who has an established herb garden in the yard. You'll quickly discover that most herb gardeners are more than willing to share divisions with you, because they're usually trying to reduce or confine their perennial holdings anyway. You're really just helping them do a bit of spring cleaning, and it's in that spirit that I suggest you offer your services.

The simplest way to obtain a division is to dig up the entire plant and then pull or tear it apart into pieces, each piece consisting of something from above ground—the plant itself—and something from below ground—the root system. Each of these pieces really constitutes a new plant, and all you have to do to make it yours is plant it in your own garden. Pack it in gently but firmly, and give it one good watering.

In early spring there's not enough growth above ground to put much of a burden on any exposed root system, but by midseason, after perennials have established leafy growth, their need of water becomes critical, so don't keep them unprotected for long. If the herbs are already more than four to six inches tall, consider yourself tardy in making the divisions. In that case take precautions. Before anything else, thoroughly water the area around the plants to be divided. After you've made your divisions, cover the exposed roots with moist soil and keep them covered in transit to their new home. After transplanting, water again. Remember, the more growth there is on top of the plant, the more important it is to keep the plant thoroughly watered until it has had a chance to re-establish itself.

Generally speaking, though, you should not attempt divisions of any perennials—peonies, phlox, or chrysanthemums, in addition to herbs—during the feverish growing periods of June, July, and August. Roots are not supporting as much growth in early spring or early fall, so that's when you should make your move.

Each perennial has its own peculiar growth pattern, so let me try to describe more precisely the dividing operation involved for the herbs in the present group.

Mint. This is the easiest plant to divide and if you fail at this, you have reason to sell the home grounds and move into an apartment. As soon as the sprouts appear, take a spade fork and loosen the soil around a grouping of them. Then shake the roots free of dirt and make your division. Be sure you have at least one sprout above ground connected to a healthy root from below ground.

Oregano. This herb sprouts up in much tighter groupings than mint does so it's a little harder to isolate and remove individual divisions. I would simply take a trowel or spade and carve out a grouping of the shoots. The soil and roots form a "plug." If you take your plug carefully, you'll find that the herb's compact root system will hold the whole grouping together for easy removal and transplanting.

Tarragon. Dig the entire plant out of the ground as soon as the new sprouts tell you where it is. Then shake all the soil free. This will reveal to you the octupuslike root system of French tarragon. Find two old stems from last year's growth and hold them firmly in each hand, then pull the whole shebang apart. Replace one half in the donor garden and save the other half for your garden. Older, more established plants will yield as many as 8 to 10 divisions.

Taking Cuttings of
Single-Stem Perennials

Group 5: SAGE

ROSEMARY

BAY

FOR A VARIETY OF REASONS, these herbs are the hardest plants for newcomers to install in their first gardens unless they are able to buy the plants outright from a professional herb grower.

There are three ways to do it on your own, and if you're just starting in herb gardening, I would try them in the following order.

First, try cluster sowing seed of each herb in February—following the techniques already given for starting chives, marjoram, and thyme from seed. If germination is achieved, transplant the strongest seedlings to individual pots.

Compared to chives, marjoram, and thyme, sage is hard to

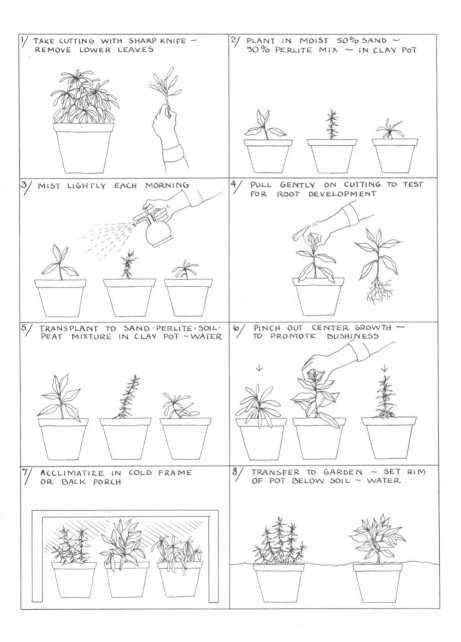

1/ TAKE CUTTING WITH SHARP KNIFE ~ REMOVE LOWER LEAVES

2/ PLANT IN MOIST 50% SAND ~ 50% PERLITE MIX ~ IN CLAY POT

3/ MIST LIGHTLY EACH MORNING

4/ PULL GENTLY ON CUTTING TO TEST FOR ROOT DEVELOPMENT

5/ TRANSPLANT TO SAND-PERLITE-SOIL-PEAT MIXTURE IN CLAY POT ~WATER

6/ PINCH OUT CENTER GROWTH ~ TO PROMOTE BUSHINESS

7/ ACCLIMATIZE IN COLD FRAME OR BACK PORCH

8/ TRANSFER TO GARDEN ~ SET RIM OF POT BELOW SOIL ~ WATER

grow from seed. Rosemary is even harder, and bay is harder still. Sage won't sprout for at least a week, rosemary for two weeks, and bay for four weeks. You may have the right soil mix and the right amount of light and moisture and still not get germination.

So, if sowing the seed fails, option two is to locate someone who is such an advanced gardener that he or she has brought these herbs indoors for winter. This may not be easy. Many people leave sage plants in the ground over winter because they're hardy. Also they zealously guard their bay plants, which are relatively sparse productions in northern areas, against any tampering. Nevertheless, if you can find someone in February or March who has all three plants in fine fettle indoors, and who is willing to let you snip a small branch off each of them, you have the means for propagating these herbs *by cutting.*

Remember, the people who are friendly enough to let you come into their herb gardens in spring to make divisions of spreading perennials will not necessarily let you hack away at the single-stem perennials they've brought indoors and carefully tended all winter long. These plants generally won't be as big or as invulnerable as the mints and such. If you don't look like you know what you're doing, their owners won't let you touch them.

The best way to take a cutting is to break off or cut off a new side shoot or the tip of the main stem of the established plant. Cut with a sharp clean knife, not a pair of scissors, which would tend to pinch or seal the end of the cutting and therefore make it harder for you to get roots from it.

The bay or sage cutting need only be an inch or two long, with two or three leaves on it. Don't just pluck off a leaf. The rosemary cutting should be a bit longer—three inches or so. Make sure some of the soft branch is included. If it's soft and greenish it means it is relatively new growth and will take favorably to rooting. If it's brown and hard—woody—don't take it because it will be too hard to root. Of the three, the bay is most likely to have been pruned and trimmed a lot and so offers little in the way of good cuttings.

Once you have your cuttings, prepare a mix of one part sand and one part perlite and pack it in an appropriate porous container such as a small clay pot or a plastic 4-by-7-inch market pack with holes in the bottom.

It's vital to use this highly drainable sand/perlite medium rather than your standard planting mix, because cuttings, without any root system at all, are susceptible to wet rot. Including soil, peat moss, or vermiculite in the mix would keep the cuttings too wet too long.

Wet the mixture and pack it down so it's good and firm. Insert the bay or sage stem a half to one inch into the mixture so it's standing erect. The leaves of rosemary grow close together so there might be 10 or 12 leaves on a three-inch cutting. Strip the leaves on the bottom ½ to ¾ inch of the stem before inserting. Any leaves left below the level of the mix would rot away, fostering a fungus condition that might spread to the stem itself.

Once you've inserted your cuttings in the pot or tray, mist daily until roots form. Do this only in early morning, never at night. You can tell roots have formed if you tug gently on the cutting and discover it tugs back. However, don't try this until two weeks after making the cutting in the case of sage, three weeks for rosemary, and at least six weeks for bay. Constant, premature tug tests will disturb the cutting unnecessarily.

Once roots are established, remove gently, shake off excess perlite and sand and transplant the cuttings to pots containing the regular soil/sand/peat moss/perlite planting mix. Soak thoroughly upon transplanting, place in a bright sunny window, and water thereafter whenever the plants look dry to the eye.

Three to five weeks after you transplant, when the plants are three to four inches high, pinch out the top center of the young seedling. This will make it bush out more effectively for a fuller, stronger plant. It will also give you another cutting if you want to start another plant. Be sure you get the stem and not just a leaf.

The hardy sage may be put out a month before the spring frost date (April 15 in my garden) provided it's been acclimatized to outdoor weather. Wait until after the last frost spring date (May 15) to put out the more tender bay and rosemary, also after acclimatizing.

If you can't borrow cuttings from someone who has sage, rosemary, and bay plants indoors, then you'll simply have to wait until June and take cuttings from established plants in the gardens of friends or neighbors—who will not mind since the herbs will be big and strong by then.

This is the third and probably most realistic way for most gardeners to get these three herbs started on their own.

The procedure for taking, rooting, and transplanting the cutting is exactly the same as we just outlined. The new plants won't have quite as long a growing season as they would if you had been able to start them from cuttings off herbs indoors, but if you get them started in June, they'll still have plenty of time to develop.

Take Your Choice

SOME OF THE HERBS included in the first herb garden plan are available in a number of different varieties, which I didn't mention earlier to avoid confusion. Actually, the range of your choice is governed by what's offered by your particular supplier of herb seed, in the case of the nine herbs we suggest starting from seed, and by whatever varieties your friends or neighbors happen to have in their gardens, in the case of the other six herbs to be propagated by division or cutting.

Anyway, let's look at the selection available among the basic cooking herbs. Sometimes there is only one standard variety. In other cases there are several to pick from. And in still others you have a veritable Baskin Robbins of choices.

Chives

Allium schoenoprasum is the standard chive for kitchen use and the one that belongs in the basic culinary garden we've described. There's a fine-leafed version also, with about the same flavor, but it gets very floppy in summer, so I don't recommend it.

Garlic chive is a productive plant with an attractive white flower, but its garlic flavor isn't what most people want in their culinary chive.

Curly chive is pretty but not nearly so productive and has maybe only 10 percent of the flavor of the standard chive. The same goes for the chives that flower in various colors.

There is also a giant chive that reaches three to four feet in height. It produces hardly any usable chive leaves and is strictly for show.

Marjoram

This herb of the oregano family has such a strong flavor that it'll hit you even before you cut it or stir it up. It has thirty or so cousins, with various different growth patterns, but none with anything like sweet marjoram's distinctive flavor. That's why even a mediocre chef insists on the real thing, *Majorana hortensis*. The hardier wild marjoram simply doesn't have the coveted strong marjoram flavor.

Thyme

There are over sixty varieties of thyme, with distinct differences in appearance, growing pattern, and flavor.

The standard cooking thyme, *Thymus vulgaris* or common thyme, grows in an erect, shrublike fashion to about twelve to fifteen inches in height.

Some thymes have un-thyme-like aromas. Caraway thyme smells like its fellow herb caraway, and orange balsam thyme and the lemon thymes have a powerful citrus flavor.

Caraway thyme and wooly thyme—so named for its fuzzy leaf—grow in creeping fashion low to the ground rather than as erect small bushes. They are often planted in and around walkways because the plants release their pleasant odors to pedestrians when trod upon. Other creepers are labeled "serpyllums" and boast pink, white, red or flesh-colored blossoms.

Certain thymes are grown mainly for their esthetic value, usually as part of a collection of a wide variety of thymes in the garden. Some of these—golden thyme and silver-edged thyme, for example—have enough flavor to be used in cooking as well.

Best bet for new gardeners: *Thymus vulgaris.*

Basil

There are a few basils to pick from.

The small-leafed variety has the strongest flavor and might be best for gourmet cooks who whip up a lot of *pesto,* the multipurpose Italian sauce.

Lettuce-leafed basil grows bigger, as the name implies, and you can begin to harvest it sooner than the other basils, but it does not have quite as strong a flavor.

Lemon-flavored basil is a pretty, erect plant that really grows more like a flower than a bush. People generally restrict its culinary use to fish dishes.

Purple- or opal-leafed basil is a must if you make basil vinegar, as it adds the right pink color to the liqiud. It's also a decorative garnish.

Sacred basil is the largest of all the basils, growing into a shrub of thirty to thirty-six inches, but is the least flavorsome.

Bush basil is a compact but productive plant growing to about twelve to fifteen inches in season, with a good strong flavor. I'd recommend it as the variety to start with. In fact, bush basil is the only type usually offered in the seed racks. If you wanted to grow any of the others from seed, you would almost certainly have to order through a catalog of an herb specialist.

Chervil

There are two basic varieties of chervil, one with a *flat* leaf, and one with a *curled* leaf. Flavor and plant size seem identical in both, so except for foliage esthetics, it really doesn't matter which you grow.

Coriander

This relative of parsley—it's known as "Indian parsley" by people who use its strong-flavored leaves in spicy Indian cuisine—exists in only one variety. Its leaves do look like parsley leaves, but its overall growth pattern is similar to that of dill and it is grown primarily for its seeds.

Parsley

Like chervil, here the basic choice is between the plain leaf and the curled leaf, only with parsley there's a wide variety within the curled-leaf group. That's because the large garnish market that exists for parsley in the restaurant trade has stimulated the development of new forms. Herbst Brothers offers five different varieties for the garnish trade and each one claims to be curlier than the one before it. They're called Double Curled, Triple Curled, Multi Curled, Optima, and Perfection.

Some of my Italian customers tell me that plain parsley is the one to grow because it has better flavor than curly, but I can't tell the difference. Either one will be perfection for the newcomer.

Mitsuba, a Japanese member of the parsley family, seems to be catching on nowadays as more people experiment with Far Eastern cooking in their kitchens. It grows two or three times bigger than our parsley and is somewhat more strongly flavored. It's easy to grow and may be ordered from many catalogs.

Dill

There are two varieties of dill worth considering, common dill and dill bouquet. Common dill grows bigger—to about three feet in my area—and produces more seedheads, but it may need staking, for if it grows too vigorously early in the season, its spindly form will be vulnerable to windy weather.

Dill bouquet is a bushier plant and does not produce seedheads in the profusion that common dill does. But if dill bouquet is planted at successive intervals in the season (as I recommend in the next chapter), it will serve your needs as well as the taller variety.

Summer Savory

There is only one summer savory though it is sometimes confused with its relative, winter savory. Summer savory is the preferred variety for the basic garden. It's bigger and better tasting and easier to grow.

Winter savory tastes the same but is not as delicate in flavor. Its one advantage over summer savory is that it is a perennial. It grows in a low bush form and can be trained for an attractive border or edging plant.

Mint

There are a couple of dozen mints, which vary in flavor and texture, in size of leaf, and in the height to which they grow.

By far the most popular mints are spearmint and peppermint. They have similar growth patterns and reach about the same height. Peppermint seems to have stronger stems, and may well produce more foliage in the growing season, though frankly I've never counted.

Spearmint is the better choice for use in cooking.

Peppermint is better for making teas—and for adding to mint juleps. We do a land office business in peppermint the first week in May every year. Hundreds of Kentucky Derby fans come by for some of this strongly flavored mint to use to cut that bourbon in the mint juleps they sip while watching the race on TV.

Oregano

We mentioned earlier that the true, pizza-quality oregano exists in only one variety, and this is the one you'll want in your first garden.

So-called wild marjoram is often sold as "oregano" by seed companies who feel free to do so because in fact the Latin name for it is *Origanum vulgare*. This is not the true oregano, which still doesn't have a proper Latin name. Wild marjoram does not have the characteristics the good cook or the average Italian is looking for. Some seed companies claim that *Origanum vulgare* is the true oregano and that if grown in a cool climate it simply does not acquire the distinctive flavor. I grow the true oregano in a cool climate and it comes out very strongly flavored.

Though the botanical jury is still out on this one, it now appears that the true oregano is not related to the marjorams as has long been believed. It is not an *Origanum* at all, but is in fact in the mint family.

Tarragon

To repeat, French tarragon, grown only from cuttings or divisions, is what we're after, and not the Russian tarragon, available in seed packets.

Sage

There are at least five hundred varieties of this most prolific of the herbs, offering a multitude of subtle differences in flavor, color, or growing and flowering habit. Technically perennials, many of the sages are too tender to survive cold winters. That's why I recommend common gray sage to most newcomers. It's got good flavor and it's hardy.

Sage is related to the popular garden flower salvia, and you'll see a fairly close resemblance between them in leaf configuration and overall growth pattern.

Rosemary

Rosemary grows in two distinctly different fashions. One variety is upright or bushlike, and the other creeps or cascades and so is more suited to hanging baskets or stone walls. Within the upright variety, there are four different types: one with blue flowers, one with white flowers, one with a bigger leaf than any of the others (called Foresty), and one with a mixed flavor (called pine-scented). With the exception of the last, all varieties, including the prostrate variety, yield the distinctive rosemary flavor desired in the kitchen.

Bay

There's only one true bay—*Laurus nobilis*. It is a full-fledged tree in its native tropical climate—growing to thirty feet in a lifetime—but in most parts of this country we know it as a mere sprig, and so value it more. A bay specimen plant of two to three feet in height in our area may take eight years to grow and will have a retail value of $100.

Maintaining the First Garden

THERE ARE A number of tricks, techniques, or procedures that can help you keep your first garden healthy and productive throughout the actual growing season. Let's look at them now.

Cultivate Ten Minutes a Week

A certain amount of weeding, by hand or with a small 3- or 4-prong hand cultivator, is required in any garden once it has been planted, though herbs pose nothing like the chore of keeping a good-sized vegetable patch clean.

It's especially important to keep the garden free of weeds early in the season. Except for the mints, most herbs are slow growers and won't be able to compete with weeds unless you help. For a 65- to 75-square-foot garden, if you devote a mere ten minutes once a week to the weeds, you should fully master them by July. The only new ones to appear after that will be random weeds that sprout from seed carried into the place by the wind, not from weed seed in the original soil mix. By that time, the herbs themselves will be fully developed and in no danger from the intruders.

Irrigate Sparingly

Herbs like it dry, remember, so wait longer than you might be inclined to wait before watering an established herb garden. There will be times in July and August, especially in a particularly dry summer, when you definitely should provide water, but if you're at all in doubt about it, test the soil first. Simply drive a spade or trowel into any bare area. If the soil is bone dry to a depth of six inches, drag out the hose or watering can. Keep foliage dry by watering gently but thoroughly at the base of the plants.

Flowers and vegetables need watering about three times as often as herbs do. There is no such thing as a "typical" summer, I suppose, but if there were, you might have to water your vegetable garden five or six times in the course of it, and your herb garden only twice.

Don't Mulch in Season

Spreading mulch material in the herb garden in an effort to suppress weeds is a bad idea because it tends to keep the soil too moist, which is just what you don't want, and also promotes fungus. An herb garden is small enough to keep weed-free by hand, no matter how busy you are with other things.

Side Dress Basil, Parsley, and Dill

These are the only three herbs in the basic garden that require a bit of extra fertilization in season to maximize their output.

If you use a liquid fertilizer like fish emulsion, or liquid seaweed, feed these herbs every two to three weeks after setting them out, or after sprouting.

If you use dried cow manure or good compost, scratch it into the soil around the plantings twice: once when the plants are four to six inches high, and again in mid-July.

Do not fertilize the other herbs in the garden or you will promote excessive leafy growth. This will diminish the manufacture of essential oils from which most herbs get their distinctive aroma and flavor. The flavor does not develop proportionately to over-stimulated leaf growth.

Other herbs that would also require a side dressing in season are the so-called salad herbs—sorrel, roquette, cress, mustard, and corn salad. These herbs, which are cut primarily for their leaves, benefit from fertilization in increased leaf production.

Pinch Out Basil

The best way to get very bushy and productive basil plants is to pinch out the top of the center stem on each plant about the time when plants are six to eight inches tall. This will prevent the plant from growing straight up, going to seed, and getting floppy, and will promote fuller growth in the lower branches. The pinching-out per se only has to be done once if you use basil regularly, because during the rest of the season, every time you harvest the basil you'll be pinching it back at the same time.

Sow Succession Crops of Dill

In order to have fresh dill on hand throughout the harvest season, make four to five sowings of dill seed, or one sowing every three weeks up until ten weeks before the fall frost date. I make my last sowing of dill on August 1 in order to harvest ripened seed prior to October 10, the average date of the first fall frost in our area.

Succession sowing of dill is especially important if you're growing cucumbers for preserving and want to use your own fresh dill in the preserving process. You can't always predict when you'll be doing your pickling, so it's better to have the seed on hand throughout. Don't forget, dill leaves add the right flavor to your pickling brew, too. Seeds are favored because they look so good inside the Mason jars.

Use a sawed-off milk carton as a frame for making the various sowings, following the outdoor sowing technique described earlier for Group 3 herbs.

Bug Problems

Insects *will* show up in an herb garden. True, most herbs are not attractive to bugs, and many herbs even repel them. But they will appear, in some seasons with more frequency than in others, and it is important to be on the alert for them every time you go out to the garden to cultivate or harvest.

First, what not to do. Because all parts of most of the herbs in the culinary garden are destined for human consumption, I strongly recommend your staying away from using any form of chemical insecticide or pesticide when bugs appear. I'd avoid using the "organic" rotenone and pyrethrum products, too. Poison is poison whether it's made in the field or the factory.

To cope with the larger forms of insects—such as the voracious caterpillar that preys on parsley, dill, and fennel and will strip those plants clean if you let it—simply hand-pick the invader and dispose of it outside the garden.

To deal with smaller insects such as white fly, spider mite, and aphid, mix a batch of Nana's Bug Juice (see page 44), and spray the invaders with that. Don't forget *under* the leaves. Include a few fresh leaves of basil in the batch for added potency.

Don't just turn your hose on such pests and spray them off, as some people have advised. Psychologically it may give you a boost to see your enemies temporarily in rout. The problem is the water pressure in your hose will knock your plants for a loop. You won't kill them, but the battering will surely set them back.

Harvesting and Storing

A LOT OF first-time herb gardeners don't realize how quickly they can start harvesting from their new plants. Within a few weeks of planting you can begin to snip from the herbs, and for the sake of productivity, you should. The more regularly you harvest throughout the summer, the more new growth you will stimulate.

Harvest with a sharp knife or pruning shears, and don't cut into any hard woody growth. If you cut two to three inches down from the tips of branches, you'll get the youngest and most flavorsome cuttings.

If and when the herbs get ahead of you—and such fast growers as oregano, chive, and basil might do that—cut them in quantity for freezing or for hanging to dry. The plants will put forth new growth in short order.

Most of the annual herbs may be harvested in quantity—cut to within 4 to 6 inches of ground level—at least twice in season, and more often if your growing season is particularly long. In taking early harvests of the annuals, don't chop them down to ground level or the plants won't recover sufficiently to give you later harvests.

Established perennials in their second or subsequent seasons can be harvested a couple of times, too. Don't cut into them too fully too late in the season, though, or they may become too weak to get through winter. Generally, never cut into the woody growth of any perennial unless you're deliberately trying to limit its growth.

The annuals and tender perennials in the herb garden should be cut prior to the first expected frost in the fall. If there's any doubt about the weather, cut the herbs down anyway as they won't grow much more thereafter even if you could get away with leaving them in for another few weeks. In the first garden, that means harvesting all the basil, chervil, and dill.

Continue to cut as needed from the hardy perennials and the biennial parsley beyond the first frost and throughout the fall. The flavor of some herbs—sage in particular—is improved by a couple of frosts, so don't turn your back on the garden just because the nights become cold. Not until you get a deep freeze, which in our area may not come until Thanksgiving, will the productive cycle of the plants come to a close for the year.

Saving Herbs for Winter

Culinary herbs can be saved for winter use in cold climates by drying, freezing, or storing in vinegar. No single way is best for all herbs. And there is no single assembly-line process for each method of preserving that works for all herbs, or for all kitchens, either. Some special harvesting and storing tips are noted for the individual culinary herbs in the Appendix. Here are general guidelines:

The best time to harvest most of the basic cooking herbs for saving, whether in dried form, frozen form or vinegars, is just before plants go into flower, because that's when oil content is highest. Two obvious exceptions are true French tarragon, which does not go into flower under any circumstances, and bay, which produces seed only in its balmy native climate. Another exception might be sweet marjoram, simply because many cooks like to take it in full flower and preserve the tiny blossoms along with the foliage. Also, if dill and coriander are being grown for their seed, then they must be taken long after the flowering process has begun, when the seed-heads start to ripen.

The best time of day to harvest for saving is late morning on a sunny day, after the dew has burned off and when the plants are at peak flavor.

Some herbs may need to be washed clean of dirt before processing, especially low and sprawling growers such as the marjoram and thyme. I know people who are so particular about their herbs that they will shake them clean rather than put them in water. If your herbs do need a rinse, use cold water, for hot water definitely does draw out the oils prematurely.

Drying is the best way to save most of the herbs, if the right conditions can be provided. An old-fashioned attic is ideal for drying herbs because it is *warm, dark, dry* and *well-ventilated.*

Herbs need warmth because that way they dry more quickly, and the faster they dry (up to a point), the better the aromatic oils are retained.

They need darkness because the absence of light keeps the herbs from losing their distinctive colors and flavors.

They must be dry and well-ventilated because both these conditions hasten the drying process and also discourage mold.

So, whether or not you have an old-fashioned attic, these are the conditions to strive for.

The herbs may be hung in small bunches to dry, or arranged in thin layers on clean paper or cookie sheets or the like, or—preferably—on screens or some mesh material to permit better air flow. Where collecting the dried seed is the object—as with dill and coriander—paper bags can be used to enclose the bunches.

Herbs dried in this manner may take from two days to two weeks to become brittle, depending on the individual herb and the actual conditions that exist.

Herbs can be dried more quickly in a kitchen oven, but care must be taken not to apply too much heat, or the aromatic oils will evaporate and some of the herbs will darken in color considerably.

"Body temperature"—98.6° Fahrenheit—is just about the perfect heat for curing most herbs. If your oven lacks a setting below 200° it may be hard to get the heat low enough even if you leave the door ajar.

It's relatively easy to cure herbs, as well as fruits and vegetables, in home food dehydrators, and with great precision. Microwave ovens have also been used for this purpose. According to one manufacturer, it takes only three to four minutes to thoroughly dry ten sprigs of any herb, with the process yielding about one to two tablespoons of the finished product.

Once dried, herbs must be stored properly or they'll lose their potency. Put them in air-tight glass jars—jars with screw-type lids

—and keep in a dark place away from excessive heat. If you can't store them in a cupboard or some other dark spot, use opaque or colored glass jars.

After drying and storing the herbs, keep checking the jars for several days to be sure no moisture appears on the inside of the glass. If this happens, it means the herbs aren't fully dry yet, and mold or fermentation will occur unless you remove them and finish the drying.

Two important additional points about dried herbs for use in cooking:

1. In dried form herbs are usually three or four times *more powerful* than in fresh form. When recipes call for a certain amount of the fresh herb, and you are using the dried herb, cut your portion to a third.

2. Most dried herbs do not retain their aroma for more than a year, even under ideal storage conditions. Dried herbs should be checked for flavor every fall and renewed from the current garden.

With some herbs, freezing works as well and in certain cases better than drying does. Some cooks claim that freezing basil, chive and parsley, in particular, is preferable to drying.

To use this technique, first wash the herbs in cold water, then let dry. Freeze the sprigs and leaves in small amounts in plastic bags. After freezing, simply use each portion as needed, dropping it into your dish frozen rather than letting it thaw.

Vinegar is another convenient and almost foolproof vehicle for carrying over the flavor of fresh herbs—especially dill, basil and tarragon—into the winter months. Most good cookbooks have plenty of simple vinegar recipes to pick from.

Even if you don't think you have the right attic or the right jars, or can't afford any of the latest labor-saving devices on the market, try drying some of your own herbs. Experiment and improvise with what you do have: you will have some success, and become much wiser for dealing with next year's harvest in the bargain.

Steps to Take for the Second Spring

AN HERB GARDEN is far from finished when the first season is over, and that's the beauty of it.

It can be brought indoors if a number of simple but carefully planned steps are taken, as we'll explain in the next chapter.

And it can be renewed with little effort in the following year—indeed the perennial herbs will renew themselves, without your assistance, if they have to.

Let's look at this schedule of activities for the second and subsequent years before considering the more complex undertaking of adopting the herbs for indoor use.

Mulch Perennials after Deep Freeze

The herb garden should be mulched at the end of the growing season to protect all the perennials, some of which are more tender than others, from a severe winter.

Mulching will also keep the herbs from coming alive prematurely during a midwinter warm spell—the January thaw we sometimes get.

Mulching is especially important if there has been a series of consecutive mild winters. Then the herbs will be acclimatized to those conditions and even more vulnerable when the hard winter comes.

The time to mulch is when the ground is frozen solid to a depth of one inch. It takes three consecutive nights in the low twenties to do it. When this happens, mulch the entire garden with a six-inch layer of salt hay, if you can obtain that superior natural insulator, or leaves, and lay some small branches or narrow boards down on top to keep the material in place.

Sow the Annuals Indoors

Beginning in February and March (for a spring frost date in May), sow seed for all annuals and other new plants indoors. Locate new and/or better sources of seed, divisions, and cuttings.

Clean Up the Garden

After all danger of a lasting snowfall is past (by the end of March in my area), remove the mulch from the herb garden.

(Leaving the mulch on too long could create a problem by heating the garden up prematurely. Some of the plants will start growing rapidly; then, when you finally remove the mulch, the new growth may have rotted for lack of light and air circulation.)

Trim off all the old growth on the perennials from which you want new shoots—namely the mint, marjoram, oregano, and tarragon. The old growth, besides looking bad, gets in the way of new growth and encourages fungus and disease. Sage and thyme plants won't need trimming, except for dead growth, because they don't die back to the ground like the others.

Move and Divide

If you want to move any of the perennials to different spots, early spring's the time to do it while the root systems are supporting relatively little growth. Maybe you put in too much of one herb last year and want to cut it back. Maybe you want to improve the esthetic or practical arrangement in the garden, or just dig and divide for the sake of doing it. Depending on your tastes, you may now want to expand a planting in one type of herb, or make some substitutions for the herbs you found you didn't use that much last year.

With the exception of mint, none of the perennials in your first garden are likely to have overreached themselves on their own by this time. In subsequent years they will though, and this early spring period would be the ideal time to tackle them.

Loosen and Replenish the Soil

Loosen the soil in the spots where this year's crop of annuals will go. Mix some good compost, rabbit manure, or dehydrated sheep or cow manure into the soil as you go. Transplant your new annuals to these spots after all danger of frost is past.

You may spot some seedlings of dill or maybe even savory. This will happen if the annuals from last year's garden were allowed to go to seed. Somehow some of the seed has survived the winter and produced new plants for you. Unless they're in the way, let them be, or move them to a more desirable location.

After the Second Year

The perennial growth in the second year will not be so great as to warrant major attention, but by the third spring, care must be taken to avoid possible overcrowded conditions. Plants will not always grow so vigorously as to interfere with the overall garden plan by the third season, but often they will. One year I built a culinary garden for one of my customers which featured a small tarragon plant in the center. The next time I stopped by was two years later, by which time the tarragon had grown four feet across and taken over virtually the whole garden.

Bear in mind that perennials by definition add to their growth every year. The very first customer I waited on as a kid needed a mature sage plant. My father directed me to one that was six years old. Its roots were so extensive it took me a half hour to dig it out. Right from the start I knew I was in a tough business.

Bringing Living Herbs Indoors

Y O U C A N G R O W all fifteen culinary herbs indoors over the winter, though with greatly reduced productivity, in the right conditions.

But you can't just dig up all the plants from your existing garden outdoors and expect them to survive among your lampshades and bookshelves.

Developing new young strong plants is really the key to having a small but vigorous herb garden inside the house over the winter months.

Also, you must have the right spot to put the herbs in their pots. If you can keep the herbs on a shelf or tray or indoor box, with a full southern exposure, then the new plants will repay the effort it took you to get them started.

Starting from Seed

Most of the herbs for indoors should be started fresh from

seed a month or two before your fall frost date—August is when we get our clay pots and seed packets out again.

Among these are all the annuals:

basil
chervil
coriander
dill
summer savory

There's no sense in trying to bring any of these indoors as potted plants directly from your garden—even though you see them flourishing out there about this time—because as annuals they will become leggy and quickly expire behind closed doors.

I also recommend starting the perennials:

sage
thyme
marjoram
chive

and the biennial:

parsley

fresh from seed.

Sage may be started from a cutting, but it's much easier to get it going from seed this time of year.

Thyme and marjoram may be started from a division, but it is not always convenient to do so either because the garden plan calls for the existing plants to spread more, or because the plants as they mature simply become too hard to divide and replant into a small pot.

Chive and parsley could be dug up and brought indoors in pots, but the pots would have to be at least six inches wide to accommodate the big root systems.

Anyway, all ten of these herbs may be started from seed using the sowing techniques described earlier.

About six to eight weeks before the frost, then, fill 4-inch clay pots with the proper mix of soil, sand, peat, and perlite, then *bury the pots up to their necks in the garden.*

Cluster sow seed for each of the herbs in these individual pots, cover with fine sand, and let germinate. Fertilize with fish emulsion or liquid seaweed when the sprouts are three to four inches high. Before the first frost they'll all be ready to come indoors as fresh herbs with lots of moderate growing ahead of them.

Starting from Division

Three of the remaining five herbs should be started from division just before frost time. These are:

mint
oregano
tarragon

After you've harvested the tops of these herbs in the fall, divide them according to the techniques described earlier for Group 4 plants, then put the divisions into 4-inch pots and *bury the pots in the ground for three good freezes.* This will give them time to recoup their energies, and prevent premature growth indoors which would weaken them. When you're ready to mulch the garden, dig out the three pots and bring them in.

There are some mints that don't take to this technique. Spearmint, curly mint, and golden mint all have the habit of losing their leaves once brought indoors, and won't revive until February. Peppermint, pineapple mint, orange mint, bergamot mint, and pennyroyal, among others, will come indoors without going into a coma.

French tarragon also becomes sickly-looking in December and starts to lose its leaves, and begins to appear a lost cause, but like the spearmint it will put forth new growth again in early February, especially if you remember it in your prayers.

Importing from the Garden

Bay and rosemary are the only herbs in our basic culinary garden that can be brought into the house for the winter as is. If you planted these in clay pots originally as suggested, all you have to do is dig them up just before the first heavy frost. If not in pots, take care in digging them up, especially the bay, which will have put down a large tap root.

If you've used 4-inch clay pots for all these procedures, you can fit all fifteen herbs into a tray or frame that measures 4 feet long by 10 inches wide by 3 to 4 inches deep. Clay pots are superior to plastic pots for indoor use because they are porous and the plants won't get waterlogged in them so easily.

With such a tray, you can construct a kind of windowbox for the inside of that picture window with your southern exposure, and have a perfect place for locating the herb garden. You can make the box out of wood and stain it or paint it to match your woodwork. More important for the herbs, you should install a leakproof metal, plastic, or aluminum-foil tray inside the box. Line this with pebbles to a depth of two inches and place your potted herbs on top of it. This will insure that, when you do water the herbs, excess moisture will find a way out of the pots.

Herb plants indoors in winter should be lightly fertilized with fish emulsion or liquid seaweed every two weeks to keep them growing well. The plants are confined in pots. They can't spread their roots out in search of food, so the food has to come to them.

Water herbs when they feel dry to the touch, but don't drown them. Overwatered herbs rot quickly.

You may have bug problems indoors, especially if you also have a profusion of house plants. Nana's Bug Juice (see page 44) works indoors as well as outdoors, though, so use it on any insects. Stay away from poisonous sprays when dealing with the edible herbs. I don't recommend washing the plants with soap and water, either, as a lot of people do. It spoils the taste of plants you're growing for the taste in the first place.

PART III

The Plans

How to Use the Plans

THE GARDEN PLANS presented in this section may be followed precisely to create your own herb garden with good results, but they are offered here mainly as examples of the rich and diverse possibilities in herb gardening. Your personal tastes and needs, as well as the special qualities and limitations of the space in which you are toiling, will determine the type of garden, or combination of gardens herein, most suitable for you. The 8-foot-by-8-foot size has been adopted purely for convenience and ease of reference in comparing the space needs and growing habits of different herbs.

A brief introduction to each plan points out any factors special to successfully growing the garden in question. For example, the Allium Garden needs a well-limed, fertilized soil for the best production. But unless otherwise noted, the general methods and conditions presented in the main text apply to all the gardens.

The herbs in each plan are listed alphabetically by popular name, along with information on their particular *life cycle, average height,* and suggested *propagation method.*

More detailed cultural information specific to each herb mentioned in this book is contained in the Herb Culture Guide at the end of the plans section. You also can find there the botanical (Latin) name for each herb.

Generally, most herbs will thrive in the growing conditions discussed in the main text. In some cases, though, additional steps are necessary to make sure an individual herb does well, and these are noted in the Herb Culture Guide where applicable. For example, several of the large-growing herbs, such as borage and lemon verbena, require a richer soil than most other herbs to do well, so we suggest composting or manuring the sections of the herb gardens where these herbs will be planted. Most perennial herbs with strong growing patterns need regular subdivision to confine them to a specific growing area. Some herbs, such as woad and St. John's Wort, are prone to prolific self-sowing and may become a nuisance in the garden. These various peculiarities are noted in the Herb Culture Guide where they apply, along with steps to take to prevent the problem.

With each plan, the *life cycle* of each herb included is given in a simple abbreviated form as follows:

A   annual

B   biennial

P   perennial

TP   tender perennial

Average height is necessarily somewhat nebulous. It means how tall a mature plant will be on about Labor Day in a typical growing season, assuming you don't live in the southern parts of Florida, Texas or California, where much greater growth will occur. If the plant is a perennial, the figure also presupposes that the plant has been properly trimmed and/or subdivided from time to time to fit its garden space.

The *propagation method* suggested for each herb in the plans is listed numerically, according to the five methods discussed in the main text:

Group 1   cluster sowing indoors
Group 2   spot sowing indoors
Group 3   cluster sowing outdoors
Group 4   root division
Group 5   stem cutting

The *bulb method* of propagation is also included to cover certain plants, mostly onions. Mainly, these are *realistic* recommendations. In some cases, the horticultural method suggested may not be the easiest, but for most gardeners it will be the most convenient. For example, we frequently suggest starting an herb from seed, either by the Group 1, 2 or 3 method, when it might be easier to propagate the herb via cutting or division, because in these cases a mature version of the plant under discussion might be hard to locate.

An asterisk (*) appears next to the names of the fifteen basic culinary herbs whenever they are used in the plans.

One more code—those herbs which are natural house plant material are shown with their *life cycle* abbreviation in brackets, such as [A], [P], or [TP]. This designation generally refers to smaller plants with relatively simple root systems, which can be contained in reasonably small pots, and which will prosper in a sunny window during the winter months. However, the code also covers such herbs as bay, eucalyptus, lemon verbena, orange osage and rosemary, which can be successfully brought indoors in tub-sized pots even as six-footers.

Each garden plan comes with an illustration showing a selection of the herbs featured in a mature state.

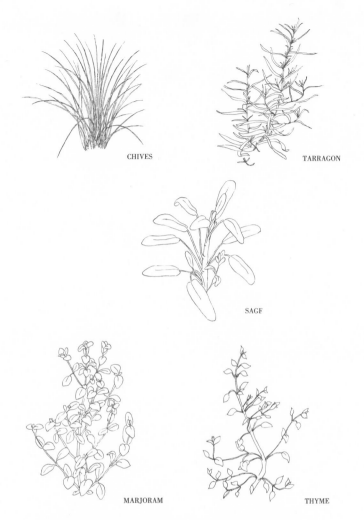

CHIVES

TARRAGON

SAGE

MARJORAM

THYME

CULINARY GARDEN—
FIRST YEAR

The fifteen basic cooking herbs have been arranged in a practical but esthetically pleasing pattern.

The tarragon plant is in the middle because it grows faster than the other perennials and so should make the best focal point.

The other perennials are placed symmetrically around the borders, where they'll be easy to get at. More important, they'll have enough room to develop in the second year.

The two mints are surrounded by Masonite boards (or some similar barrier) sunk to a depth of ten to twelve inches, which should keep their fast-growing root systems in place.

The annual herbs (with the exception of the chervil) are set in an inner circle around the tarragon. Flat stepping stones have been dropped in the garden to provide easy access to the annuals in the middle.

At season's end, the bay and rosemary have to be brought inside in pots, since they will not survive the winter outside, at least not in northern regions. The chives should be cut back at season's end. Harvest all annuals one last time just before the first frost. Pull up their root systems and remove them to keep the garden clean.

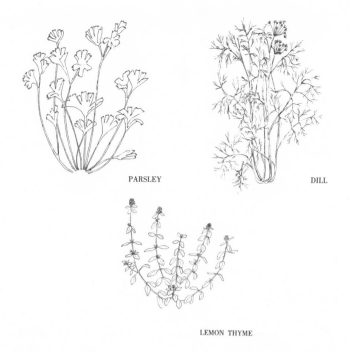

PARSLEY

DILL

LEMON THYME

SUMMER SAVORY

CHERVIL

CULINARY GARDEN— SECOND YEAR

To restore the garden population to normal, resow or replant all the annuals, and bring out the rosemary and bay from indoors. Transplant these last two into slightly larger pots, then bury them in the pots in the garden.

The biennial parsley will grow rapidly early in the second season. Harvest it promptly and often, to delay its going to seed. Dig up one or more of your existing parsley plantings, and sow new parsley for a fresh crop to replace the first year's crop. Remove the old parsley completely by late spring as its life cycle is now over. The deep tap roots on the parsley plants require digging out with a spade, rather than simply uprooting by hand. By this time the new parsley should be well established.

Watch for unwanted volunteers appearing early in spring in the spots where last year's dill, coriander and chervil grew, and also around oregano and marjoram, the two perennials with a knack for dropping seed. Self-sowing will occur more often in a garden which was not assiduously harvested, and in a garden which was well mulched for winter—the mulch protects the fallen seed from the winter.

This particular garden doesn't depend on the herbs to self-sow, but if it happens, and you have room to accommodate the seedlings where they are, or even elsewhere (though remember, these annuals do not transplant well), by all means keep them.

At the *end* of the second season:

Bring the bay and rosemary back indoors in their pots. If they have put on a lot of growth during the season, transplant them into larger pots—but not too much larger. Generally, don't increase pot diameter by more than two inches in a season.

Dig up the tarragon, reduce and relocate where the bay grew. (In its place next year, put the rosemary, which by then will have become the larger and more attractive center plant.)

Divide and reduce the chives and mints, if they're getting too big.

Confine the root systems of the oregano and marjoram by trimming with a sharp edging tool, removing the unwanted peripheral roots and refilling those areas with fresh compost or soil.

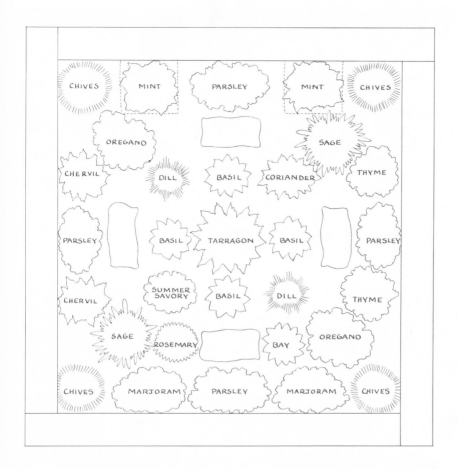

Clip the branches of the sage, if that plant has gotten too big for its assigned place.

Do the same for the thyme. If it has flopped over and taken root beyond its borders, spade out the unwanted portions. Any excess can be used as filler in a rock garden or patio area, or any other appropriate spot on the grounds.

110

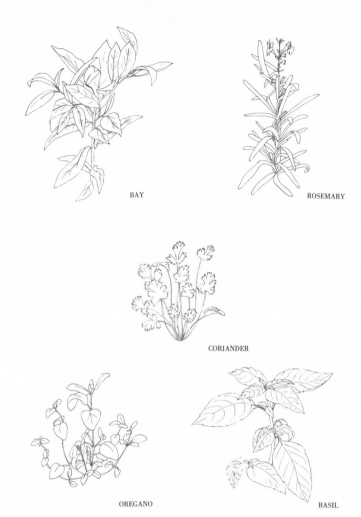

BAY

ROSEMARY

CORIANDER

OREGANO

BASIL

CULINARY GARDEN—
THIRD YEAR

Now tasks become more familiar as they begin to repeat themselves.

The rosemary comes back outdoors, this time to center stage in the garden. It should be nearly two feet high and twelve to fourteen inches wide.

The bay comes back outdoors.

Replant annuals.

Keep the established parsley cut back; sow fresh parsley as in preceding year.

If any end-of-second-year tasks described earlier were not completed, do them now at the beginning of the third year:

—Dig up and replant in smaller forms the chives, mints and tarragon. By this time, they surely will have spread too much for the limited space available to them in this garden.

—Renew your thyme, as older woody plants don't produce the tender leaves desirable in cooking.

By the end of this third year in the garden, you will know the needs of your plants and your own needs well enough to handle things smoothly and at precisely the right time.

*BASIL	A	18″	2
*BAY	[TP]	2–6′	5
*CHERVIL	A	24″	2
*CHIVES	P	12″	1
*CORIANDER	A	24″	2
*DILL	A	30″	3
*MARJORAM	TP	12″	1
*OREGANO	P	24″	4
*PARSLEY	B	8″	3
*ROSEMARY	[TP]	4′	5
*SAGE	P	24″	5
*SPEARMINT	P	18″	4
*SUMMER SAVORY	A	18″	3
*TARRAGON	P	30″	4
*THYME	P	12″	1

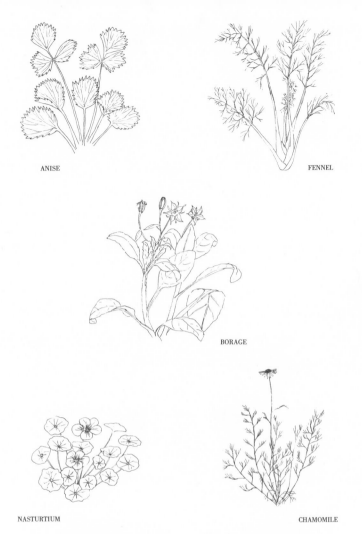

ANISE

FENNEL

BORAGE

NASTURTIUM

CHAMOMILE

ANNUAL GARDEN

This plan is given mainly to show the most popular annual varieties at a glance. However, it could also be used by people who are
not able to garden in the same location for more than one year.
The nasturtium and the versatile basil have been planted in quantity because they make nice rows. The borage provides a good
centerpiece because of its upright growth and pretty blue flowers.
The entire garden could be planted in one day, with the exception
of basil, if there is still a chance of cold nights.

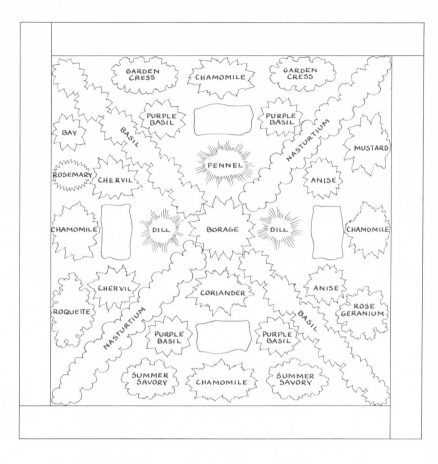

ANISE	A	24″	3
*BASIL	A	18″	2
BORAGE	A	30″	2
CHAMOMILE	A	18″	2
*CHERVIL	A	24″	2
*CORIANDER	A	24″	2
CRESS	A	6″	3
*DILL	A	30″	3
FENNEL	A	30″	3
MUSTARD	A	18″	3
NASTURTIUM	A	8″	3
PURPLE BASIL	A	18″	2
ROQUETTE	A	10″	3
ROSE GERANIUM	A	24″	5
*SUMMER SAVORY	A	18″	3

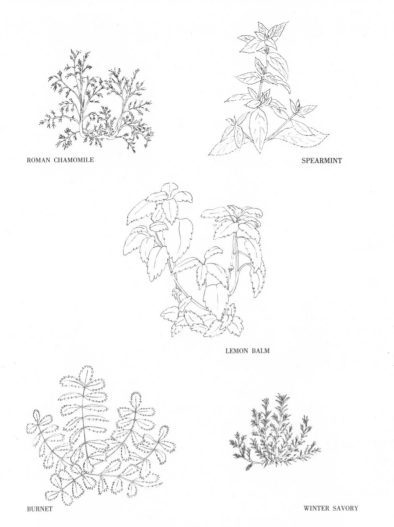

ROMAN CHAMOMILE

SPEARMINT

LEMON BALM

BURNET

WINTER SAVORY

PERENNIAL GARDEN

Here's a plan for people who don't want to fuss with annuals every year. By the end of the first season, the majority of the herbs here will have established a full and vigorous growth pattern. During the second year, the bay, rosemary, thyme and winter savory will have done the same. Early in the second year, the sorrel should be watched carefully because it tends to get big and floppy. If you trim it continuously beginning early in the second year, it will keep its place.

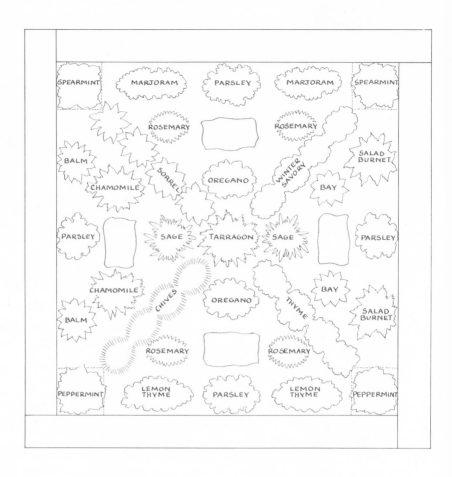

*BAY	[TP]	2–6′	5
BURNET	P	18″	2
*CHIVES	P	12″	1
LEMON BALM	P	18″	4/2
*MARJORAM	TP	12″	1
MINTS: PEPPERMINT/	P	24″	4
*SPEARMINT	P	18″	4
*OREGANO	P	24″	4
ROMAN CHAMOMILE	P	6″	1
*ROSEMARY	[TP]	4′	5
*SAGE	P	24″	5
SORREL	P	18″	3
*TARRAGON	P	30″	4
*THYME	P	12″	4
GERMAN THYME	P	12″	1
LEMON THYME	P	4″	4
WINTER SAVORY	P	12″	2

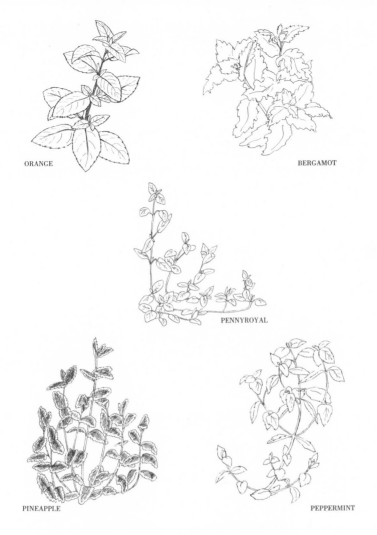

ORANGE

BERGAMOT

PENNYROYAL

PINEAPPLE

PEPPERMINT

MINT GARDEN

This plan is for people who want the full range of mint flavors. Installing the extra dividers (I've used railroad ties cut to size) is a bother initially, but it pays off over the years. It's the only sane way to grow a variety of mints in the same bed.

Keep cutting back all the mints throughout the growing season. If you let two or more go to flower, the bees will cause cross-pollination and your varieties will get even more varied. Harvest four

to six inches off the stems every other week during the summer. If you can't use all the clippings immediately, hang them to dry, then store in glass jars in a dark closet. They'll last through winter for all your mint needs.

The drawback to continuous cutting is that it stimulates root growth in plants that naturally spread like wildfire in the first place. In two or three years, each mint will become overcrowded in its two-foot-by-two-foot growing area and needs to be subdivided and started anew.

There are dozens of different varieties of mint. The ones included here have been most popular among my customers, who use them chiefly in teas, cold drinks, fruit salads and jellies.

APPLE	P	24″	4
BERGAMOT	P	18″	4
CURLY	P	24″	4
GOLDEN	P	18″	4
ORANGE	P	24″	4
PENNYROYAL	P	3″	3
PEPPERMINT	P	24″	4
PINEAPPLE	P	12″	4
*SPEARMINT	P	18″	4

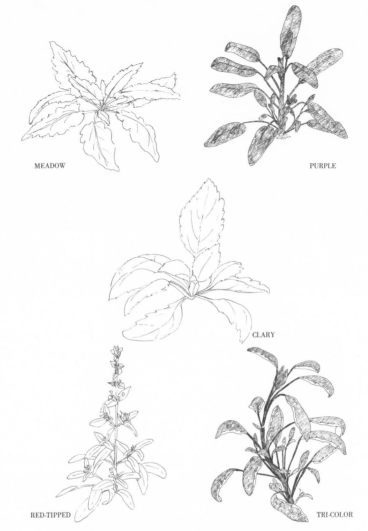

MEADOW

PURPLE

CLARY

RED-TIPPED

TRI-COLOR

SAGE GARDEN

Sage is a natural collector's item because it comes in so many
varieties (there are at least 500 known members of the species)
and offers so many contrasts in color of foliage and flower. Many
of the varieties also tend to "sport"-- ⸱ horticultural quirk whereby
different colors appear in leaves or flowers on the same plant.
Every year I get at least one common gray sage that is gray-green
on one side of the leaf, as it is supposed to be, and pure white on
the other, as though someone had touched it up with a paintbrush.

The sages included in this plan are among the showiest of those varieties that are most readily available.

Most sages get big quickly, which is why they are given so much garden space here. They must also be trimmed from time to time, especially after the second season, when unchecked growth would diminish the esthetic effect of this garden.

In propagating the golden, purple and tri-color from cuttings, pick sprigs with the most desirable color variation in their leaves, so that this characteristic carries over into the new plant.

*SAGE	P	24″	5
CLARY	B	4′	2
DWARF	[TP]	8″	5
GOLDEN	P	15″	5
MEADOW	P	30″	2
PINEAPPLE	TP	30″	5
PURPLE	P	15″	5
RED-TIPPED	A	15″	2
TRI-COLOR	P	15″	5

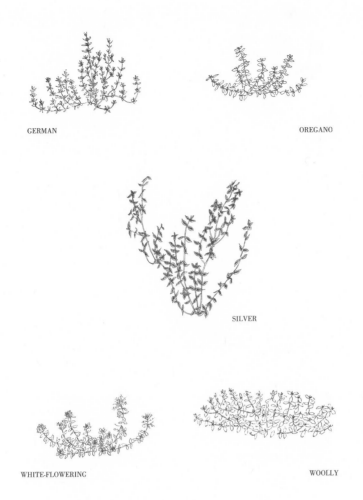

GERMAN

OREGANO

SILVER

WHITE-FLOWERING

WOOLLY

THYME GARDEN

The clock pattern of this plan takes several years to fully develop, and needs a lot of attention to trimming. Three low-growing creeping varieties—woolly, white-flowering and golden—have been used to define the main areas. Bricks could be used to frame the clockface from the start; otherwise trim and train the woolly and white-flowering thymes to get the same effect gradually.

The clock can be "set" for any time, of course—the hour of a special birth, say, or some other cherished occasion.

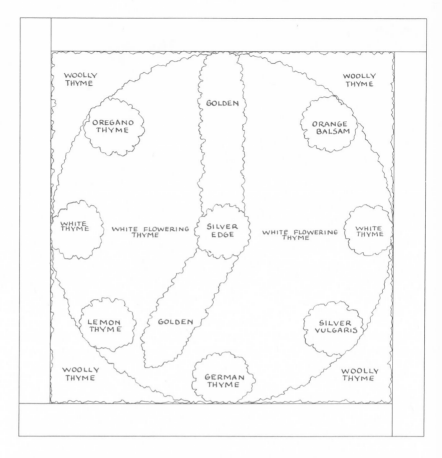

Most thymes are perennials, but there are variations in their degree of hardiness, so it's a good idea to winter-mulch the entire thyme garden in northern areas.

It's possible to start most thymes from seed if you can find the seed, but with the exception of common thyme, this would not be easy, so we recommend propagation by division or cutting. In cases where the color or color variegation is a special feature, take cuttings that best represent that feature.

Woolly thyme varieties are especially prone to fungus disease in wet periods. If your plants start rotting, cut them back severely to promote new, healthy growth.

Thyme is one of the three or four most popular herbs to grow. If you're going to try to build a collection of thymes, though, be prepared for a challenge and some frustration, because there is rampant confusion in the naming and labeling of the varieties. I've ordered what turned out to be the same variety of thyme under six or seven different names on several occasions. This is partly due to the subtle ways in which many of the varieties differ. In fact in twenty years of growing the herb, I myself think I have finally learned to recognize and identify for certain only about twenty varieties.

*THYME	P	12″	1
GERMAN	P	12″	1
GOLDEN	[P]	8″	5
LEMON	P	4″	4
ORANGE BALSAM	P	8″	5
OREGANO	P	8″	5
SILVER	[P]	8″	5
COMMON SILVER	[P]	8″	5
WHITE-FLOWERING	P	1″	4
WOOLLY	P	1″	4

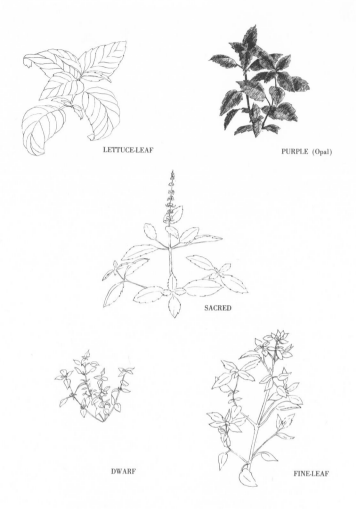

LETTUCE-LEAF

PURPLE (Opal)

SACRED

DWARF

FINE-LEAF

BASIL GARDEN

Here's the perfect garden for supplying all the basil a small Italian restaurant would need. Actually, most traditional Italian families with garden space grow at least a half-dozen basil varieties. Few Italians seem to agree as to which variety makes the best *pesto* sauce, however. I've learned to stay out of arguments on the subject, but when pressed, over a glass of home-made red wine, I usually say that the smaller the basil leaf, the better the *pesto* flavor.

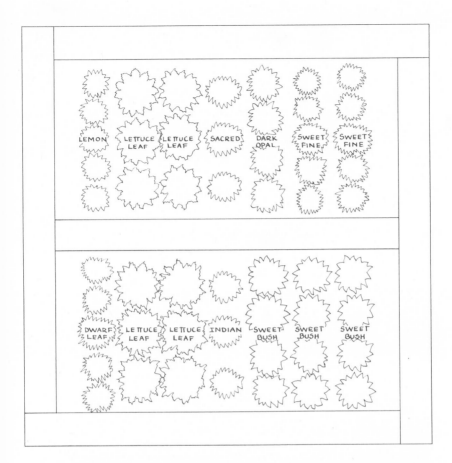

In this plan the basils have been arranged in rows, crop-style, with the tall-growing sacred and Indian varieties in the middle.

Among the small-leafed basils (bush, dwarf and fine leaf) there is always some variation in growth pattern. If I were to raise a dozen plants of one type from the seeds, I'd seldom get more than three plants that look exactly alike. They'll range in leaf length from one-eighth to three-eighth inch and in height from six inches to fourteen inches.

*BASIL (Common or Bush)	A	18″	2
DWARF	A	12″	2
FINE-LEAF	A	15″	2
INDIAN	A	24″	2
LEMON	A	15″	2
LETTUCE-LEAF	A	18″	2
PURPLE (Opal)	A	18″	2
SACRED	A	30″	2

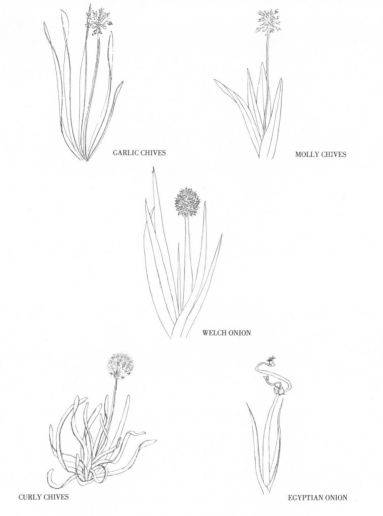

GARLIC CHIVES

MOLLY CHIVES

WELCH ONION

CURLY CHIVES

EGYPTIAN ONION

ALLIUM GARDEN

The lowly onion can make one of the most attractive and easy-to-care-for gardens of all. This one is arranged crop-style, with the four-foot high gigantium in the corners. Started from bulbs or seedlings, the chive, molly, Welch onion, and roseum are allowed to flower in purple, yellow, white and pink, respectively.

The gigantium, molly and roseum are mainly decorative and are usually not used in cooking.

The leeks and onions are harvested in full in the fall and need to be replaced with new crops in the spring.

The onion family grows much better in a sweet, moderately enriched soil. This garden should be well-limed and composted or manured for maximum productivity.

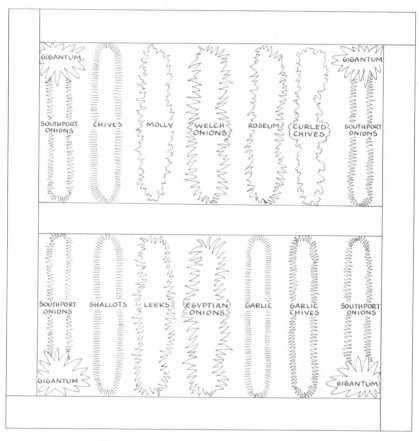

CHIVES	P	12″	1		GARLIC	P	24″	
OTHER CHIVES:					LEEKS	P	24″	
CURLY	P	6″	4		ONIONS	B	18″	
GARLIC	P	12″	4		EGYPTIAN	P	24″	
GIGANTIUM	P	36″	Bulb		WELCH	P	18″	4
MOLLY	P	15″	Bulb		SHALLOTS	P	15″	
ROSEUM	P	12″	Bulb					

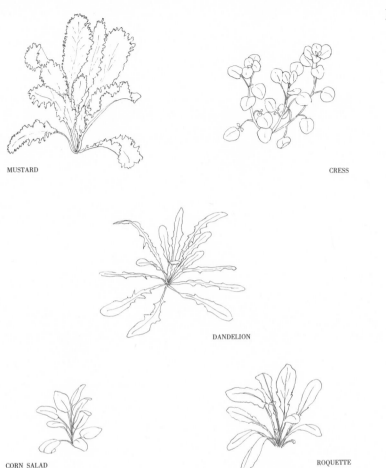

MUSTARD

CRESS

DANDELION

CORN SALAD

ROQUETTE

SALAD GARDEN

The salad herbs have been planted in rows rather than spot-planted, so this looks more like a vegetable garden than an herb garden. Annuals and perennials are separated by the divider. The sorrel, roquette, cress and dandelion can be used in place of lettuce as well as with lettuce in many salads. The other herbs are used to accent salads and a lot of other dishes, too. Make sure to keep picking salad herbs during the summer so they don't go to

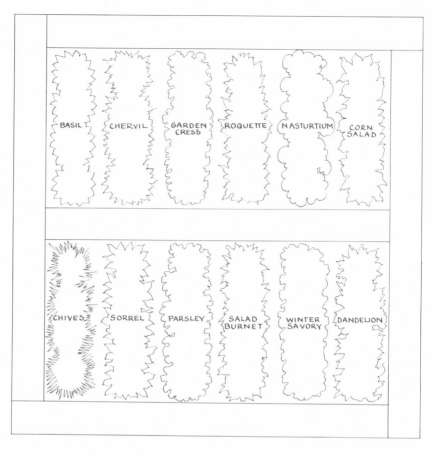

seed. If any of the annuals get ahead of you and begin to toughen, pull them up and sow new seed.

*BASIL	A	18″	2
BURNET	P	18″	2
*CHIVES	P	12″	1
CORN SALAD	A	8″	3
CRESS	A	6″	3
DANDELION	P	4″	3
MUSTARD	A	18″	3
NASTURTIUM	A	8″	3
*PARSLEY	B	8″	3
ROQUETTE	A	10″	3
SORREL	P	18″	3
WINTER SAVORY	P	12″	2

BORAGE

CARAWAY

BEE BALM

CALENDULA

CATNIP

TEA GARDEN

Many more herbs can be used to make teas than the ones given in this plan; the type and quantity of the selection here simply reflects our own tea tastes. Comfrey, hyssop, lemon verbena and dozens of other herbs are also quite popular. Generally, use a tablespoon of fresh herbs (or a teaspoon of dried herbs) per cup of boiling water, and steep for about ten minutes. Blends of herbs can also be as tasty as single-herb teas.

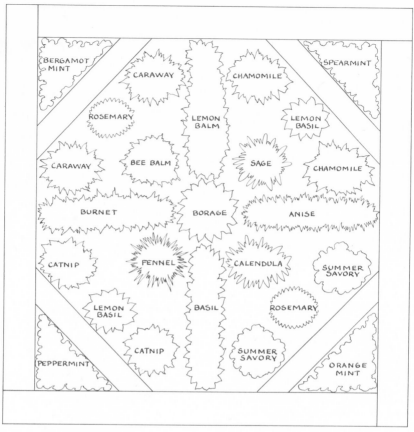

ANISE	A	24″	3
BEE BALM	P	30″	4
BORAGE	A	30″	2
BURNET	P	18″	2
CALENDULA	A	24″	2/3
CHAMOMILE	A	18″	2
CARAWAY	B	24″	2
CATNIP	P	18″	1/4
FENNEL	A	30″	3
LEMON BALM	P	18″	4/2
LETTUCE-LEAF BASIL	A	18″	2
MINTS:			
BERGAMOT	P	18″	4
ORANGE	P	24″	4
PEPPERMINT	P	24″	4
*SPEARMINT	P	18″	4
*ROSEMARY	[TP]	4′	5
*SAGE	P	24″	5
*SUMMER SAVORY	A	18″	3

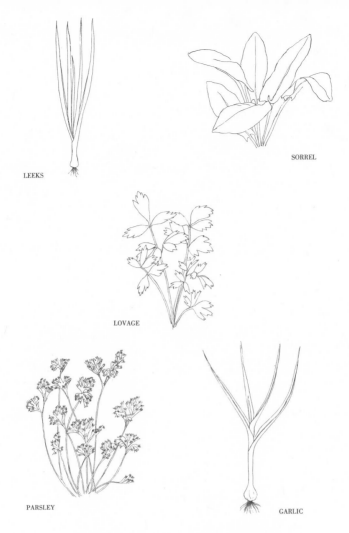

LEEKS

SORREL

LOVAGE

PARSLEY

GARLIC

SOUP GARDEN

These are the most popular herbs used in making and seasoning soups among my customers. The lovage in the center will grow up to six feet even if you keep trimming it, so if you're not sure you'll use this herb, eliminate it as a center plant and fill in with more sorrel instead.

*BASIL	A	18″	2
*BAY	[TP]	2–6′	5
BORAGE	A	30″	2
CARAWAY	B	24″	2
*CHIVES	P	12″	1
*DILL	A	30″	3
GARLIC	P	24″	Bulb
LEEKS	P	24″	1
LEMON BALM	P	18″	4/2
LOVAGE	P	6′	2
*MARJORAM	TP	12″	1
*PARSLEY	B	8″	3
*ROSEMARY	[TP]	4′	5
*SAGE	P	24″	5
SORREL	P	18″	3
*TARRAGON	P	30″	4
*THYME	P	12″	1
WINTER SAVORY	P	12″	2

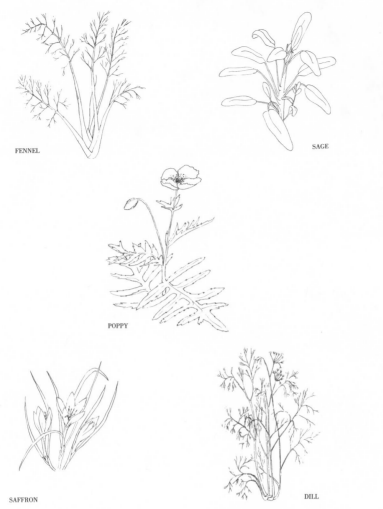

FENNEL

SAGE

POPPY

SAFFRON

DILL

BREAD GARDEN

Only a small quantity of any of these herbs, fresh or dried, is needed to give a delightful flavor to loaves of home-baked bread.

The rows of saffron, or autumn crocus, can make this a lovely and enduring garden. In the first year, start everything except the saffron in the spring. Then, around Labor Day, plant the saffron from bulbs, which will be readily available in good garden centers at that time. In about six weeks, the saffron will flower, and you can collect the precious orange stigmas, which are used for

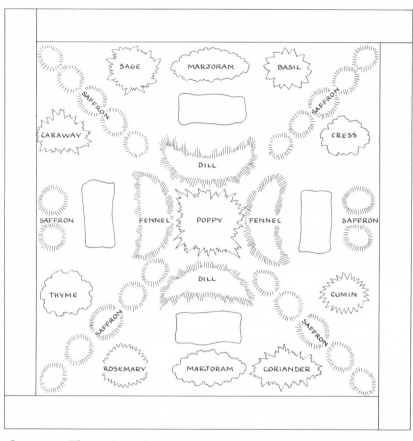

flavoring. Thereafter, the saffron will flower beautifully every fall without any more work on your part.

CARAWAY	B	24″	2
*CORIANDER	A	24″	2
CRESS	A	6″	3
CUMIN	A	8″	2
*DILL	A	30″	3
FENNEL	A	30″	3
FINE-LEAF BASIL	A	15″	2
*MARJORAM	TP	12″	1
POPPY	A	36″	2
*ROSEMARY	[TP]	4′	5
SAFFRON	P	8″	Bulb
*SAGE	P	24″	5
*THYME	P	12″	1

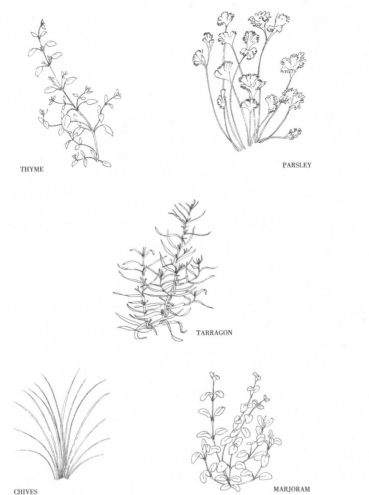

THYME

PARSLEY

TARRAGON

CHIVES

MARJORAM

BREAKFAST GARDEN

For lovers of omelettes (or scrambled eggs), here is a garden that will permit great variety in the flavor of your breakfasts and brunches. It doubles as a salad garden.

*CHIVES	P	12″	1
CRESS	A	6″	3
CUMIN	A	8″	2
*DILL	A	30″	3
DWARF BASIL	A	12″	2
*MARJORAM	TP	12″	1
MUSTARD	A	18″	3
ONIONS	B	18″	Bulb
*PARSLEY	B	8″	3
*ROSEMARY	[TP]	4′	5
*SUMMER SAVORY	A	18″	3
*TARRAGON	P	30″	4
*THYME	P	12″	1

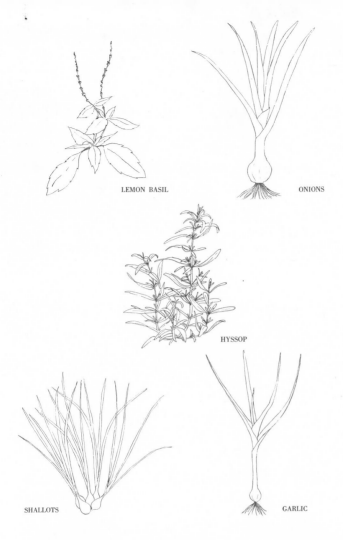

LEMON BASIL

ONIONS

HYSSOP

SHALLOTS

GARLIC

FISH & GAME GARDEN

Here's a functional layout of the herb seasonings most commonly used to temper strong-tasting fish dishes and meals made from wild fowl, venison and such.

*BAY	[TP]	2–6′	5
*DILL	A	30″	3
FENNEL	A	30″	3
GARLIC	P	24″	Bulb
HYSSOP	P	24″	2
LEMON BASIL	A	15″	2
*MARJORAM	TP	12″	1
MUSTARD	A	18″	3
ONIONS	B	18″	Bulb
*OREGANO	P	24″	4
*PARSLEY	B	8″	3
*ROSEMARY	[TP]	4′	5
*SAGE	P	24″	5
SHALLOTS	P	15″	Bulb
*SUMMER SAVORY	A	18″	3
*TARRAGON	P	30″	4
*THYME	P	12″	1

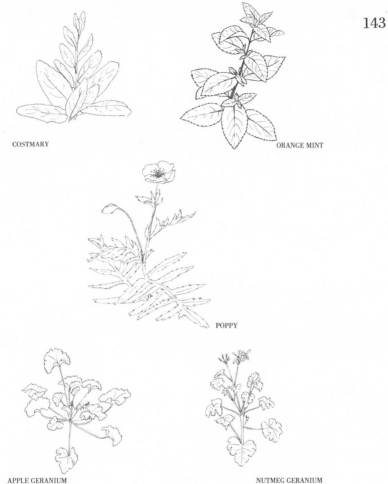

COSTMARY

ORANGE MINT

POPPY

APPLE GERANIUM

NUTMEG GERANIUM

CAKE & COOKIE GARDEN

This plan contains the herbs whose leaves and seeds are frequently
used as ingredients in dessert dishes.

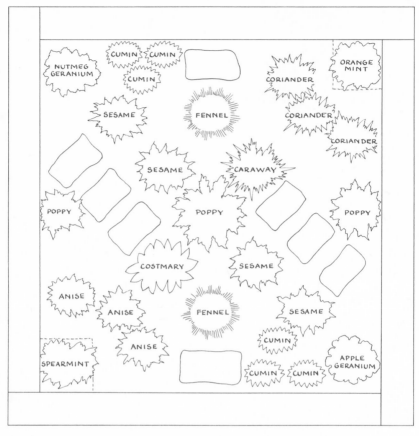

ANISE	A	24″	3
CARAWAY	B	24″	2
*CORIANDER	A	24″	2
COSTMARY	P	36″	4
CUMIN	A	8″	2
FENNEL	A	30″	3
MINTS:			
ORANGE	P	24″	4
*SPEARMINT	P	18″	4
POPPY	A	36″	2
SCENTED GERANIUMS:			
APPLE	[A]	12″	5
NUTMEG	[A]	18″	5
SESAME	A	18″	2

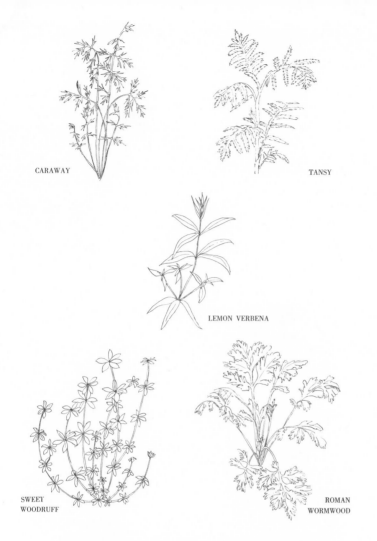

CARAWAY

TANSY

LEMON VERBENA

SWEET
WOODRUFF

ROMAN
WORMWOOD

HOME BAR GARDEN

This might be a popular garden off a porch or patio for folks who make libations an important part of their entertaining. Some of these herbs are best used fresh to flavor iced drinks; others are traditionally used to give distinctive tastes to home-made wines and liqueurs.

The mints and lemon verbena should be confined, or may be raised in large containers like old whiskey barrels partly to convey the personality of the garden, but also to help those herbs

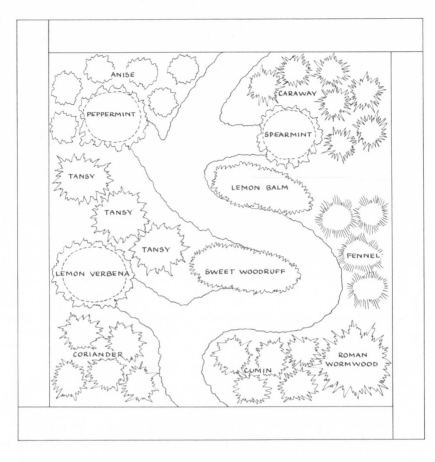

grow their best. The sweet woodruff in the center will do well only if something like a barrel or umbrella is there to keep it shaded; otherwise you should plant this May wine ingredient in a naturally shady spot.

ANISE	A	24″	3
CARAWAY	B	24″	2
*CORIANDER	A	24″	2
CUMIN	A	8″	2
FENNEL	A	30″	3
LEMON BALM	P	18″	4/2
LEMON VERBENA	[A]	6′	5
MINTS:			
PEPPERMINT	P	24″	4
*SPEARMINT	P	18″	4
ROMAN WORMWOOD	P	18″	4
SWEET WOODRUFF	P	12″	4/5
TANSY	P	36″	4

EUCALYPTUS

AMBROSIA

ROSE

VIOLETS

SWEET MYRTLE

POTPOURRI GARDEN

The emphasis in this plan is on the herbs most frequently used in making dried potpourris. Leaves (and rose petals) should be harvested, dried and stored in a sealed, opaque container. If a few drops of fixative are added, the mixture will retain its potency much longer.

A hybrid tea rose would be the best choice for the center plant here; other types of roses get too big for the space available.

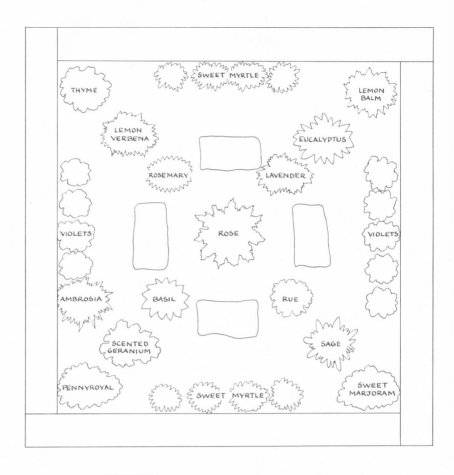

AMBROSIA	A	18″	2/3
*BASIL	A	18″	2
EUCALYPTUS	[TP]	6′	2
LAVENDER VERA	P	18″	2/5
LEMON BALM	P	18″	4/2
LEMON VERBENA	[A]	6′	5
*MARJORAM	TP	12″	1
ORANGE BALSAM THYME	P	8″	5
PENNYROYAL MINT	P	3″	3
ROSE	P	5′	–
ROSE GERANIUM	A	24″	5
*ROSEMARY	[TP]	4′	5
RUE	P	24″	2
SWEET MYRTLE	[TP]	18″	5
VIOLETS	P	4″	3/4

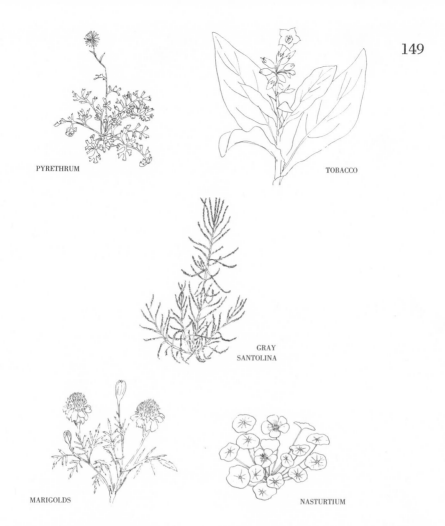

PYRETHRUM

TOBACCO

GRAY
SANTOLINA

MARIGOLDS

NASTURTIUM

PEST REPELLANT GARDEN

Here are some herbs frequently used in "companion-planting" to deter pests in vegetable gardens. I'm not an advocate of companion-planting in vegetable plots of limited space, simply because the method robs crop space. But I do believe in the underlying principle and in fact make my own organic pesticides by harvesting the leaves and/or flowers of the herbs featured, chopping them in a blender, letting the concoction sit overnight in some water, then straining and spraying on the plants with the bug problems.

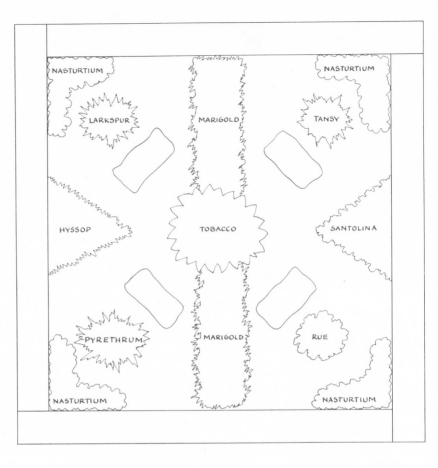

DETERS:

GRAY				
SANTOLINA	P	12″	5	*aphid, white fly*
HYSSOP	P	24″	2	*white fly*
LARKSPUR	A	30″	2	*aphid*
MARIGOLDS	A	15″	2	*nematodes*
NASTURTIUM	A	8″	3	*beetles*
PYRETHRUM	P	18″	2	*mites, aphid,*
				leafhopper
RUE	P	24″	2	*beetles*
TANSY	P	36″	4	*ants*
TOBACCO	A	5′	2	*aphid*

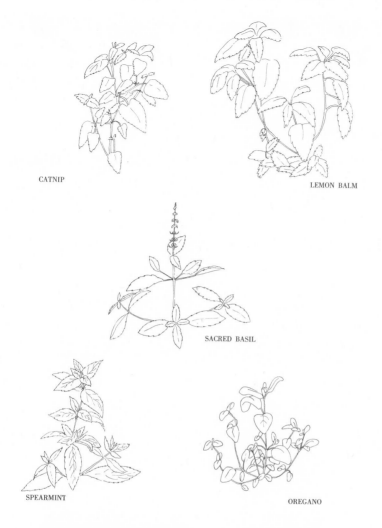

CATNIP

LEMON BALM

SACRED BASIL

SPEARMINT

OREGANO

HONEYBEE GARDEN

These most aromatic herbs are favorites of bees and beekeepers. The borage areas should be sown in succession, at about two-week intervals, to maximize the appeal of that herb's blossoms for bees. All the other plants in the garden should be chopped back as soon as the blooms begin to fade and fall—to encourage new flowering and continued bee traffic.

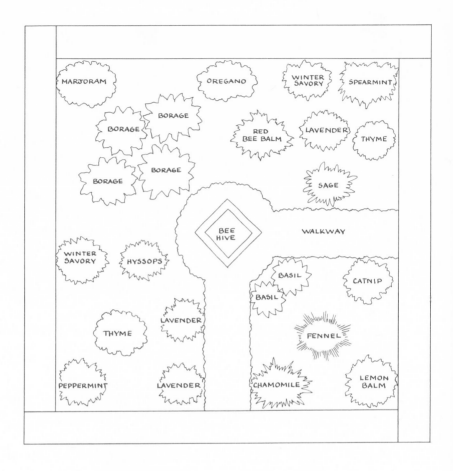

BEE BALM	P	30″	4
BORAGE	A	30″	2
CHAMOMILE	A	18″	2
CATNIP	P	18″	1/4
FENNEL	A	30″	3
HYSSOP	P	24″	2
LAVENDER MUNSTEAD	P	15″	2/5
LEMON BALM	P	18″	4/2
*MARJORAM	TP	12″	1
MINTS:			
PEPPERMINT	P	24″	4
*SPEARMINT	P	18″	4
*OREGANO	P	24″	4
*SAGE	P	24″	5
SACRED BASIL	A	30″	2
*THYME	P	12″	1
WINTER SAVORY	P	12″	2

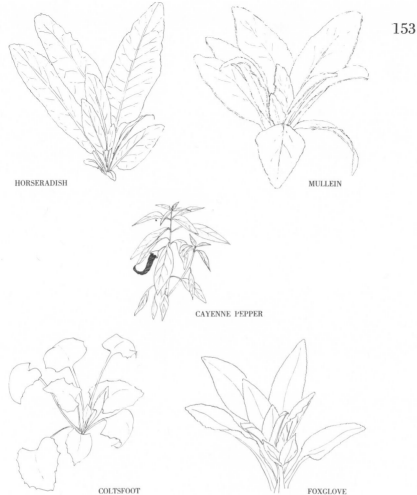

HORSERADISH

MULLEIN

CAYENNE PEPPER

COLTSFOOT

FOXGLOVE

MEDICAL HERB GARDEN

This plan consists of some of the herbs used in remedies for virtually anything that ails you. It amounts to a kind of backyard pharmacy.

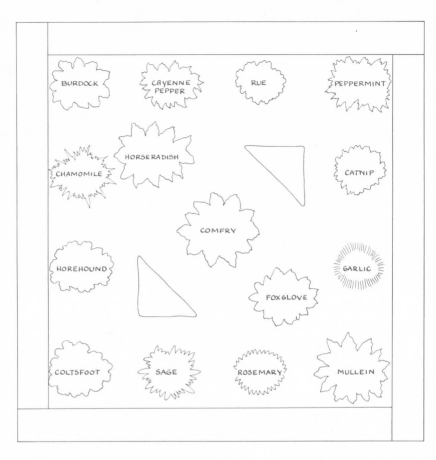

BURDOCK	B	36″	3
CHAMOMILE	A	18″	2
CATNIP	P	18″	1/4
CAYENNE PEPPER	A	30″	2
COLTSFOOT	P	12″	3/4
COMFREY	P	36″	4
FOXGLOVE	B	36″	2
GARLIC	P	24″	Bulb
HOREHOUND	P	18″	2
HORSERADISH	P	24″	4
MULLEIN	B	6′	2
PEPPERMINT	P	24″	4
*ROSEMARY	[TP]	4′	5
RUE	P	24″	2
*SAGE	P	24″	5

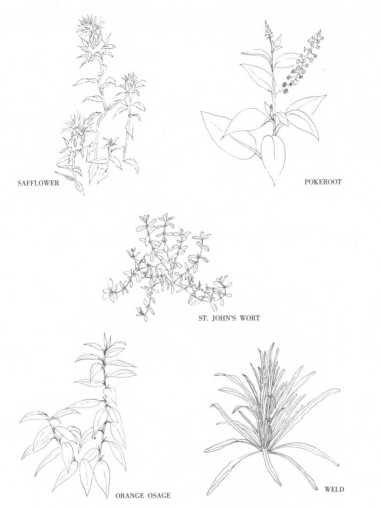

SAFFLOWER

POKEROOT

ST. JOHN'S WORT

ORANGE OSAGE

WELD

DYER'S GARDEN

There has been a tremendous increase in interest in using natural colors among people who make their own clothes and textiles. A representative selection of herbs that can be easily grown for dyeing purposes are in this plan. All the plants here grow big and tall, so no particular effort has been made to "design" the garden. Yet this or any garden of dye plants will be most attractive.

Here are some good dye sources for specific colors from

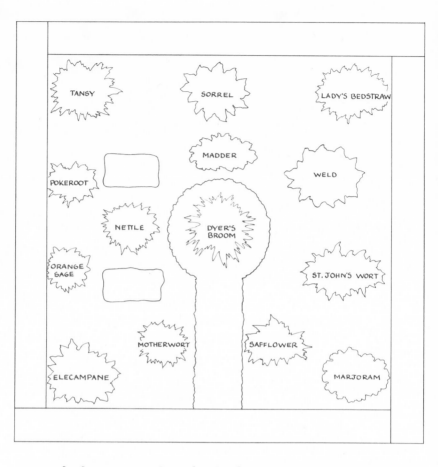

among herbs mentioned in this book (not all of them appear in this particular garden):

YELLOW
  lady's bedstraw
  dyer's broom
  dyer's chamomile
  safflower
  saffron
  St. John's Wort
  weld

GREEN
  motherwort

RED
  lady's bedstraw (roots)
  madder
  rue (roots)
  wild marjoram

DARK YELLOW/GOLD
marigolds

TAN/GOLD
orange osage

BRASS/BURNT ORANGE
onion

YELLOW/GREEN
tansy
nettle
sorrel

BLUE
woad
elecampane

MAGENTA
dandelion

DYER'S BROOM	P	18″	2
ELECAMPANE	P	4′	4
LADY'S BEDSTRAW	P	24″	2
MADDER	P	12″	4
MOTHERWORT	P	30″	2
NETTLE	P	36″	3
ORANGE OSAGE	[P]	6′	2
POKEROOT	P	4′	2
ST. JOHN'S WORT	P	18″	3
SAFFLOWER	A	24″	2
SORREL	P	18″	3
TANSY	P	36″	4
WELD	A	24″	3
WILD MARJORAM	P	18″	1

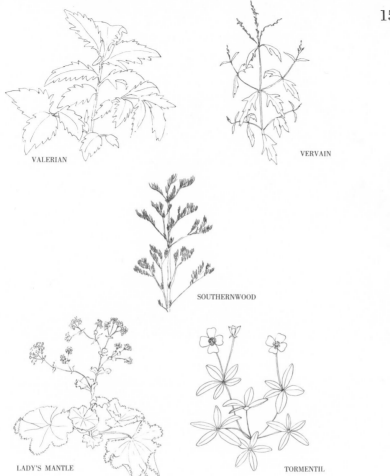

VALERIAN

VERVAIN

SOUTHERNWOOD

LADY'S MANTLE

TORMENTIL

APHRODISIAC GARDEN

I can't swear by the effectiveness of any of the herbs given here, which figure in many traditional love potions or rituals designed to gain the favor of a loved one. I do know for a fact that my wife's grandfather ate two garlic cloves a day all his life, and fathered seventeen children. I also have seen rosemary render young females a bit silly and perhaps vulnerable. One Christmas season I hired several young women to make a large quantity of holiday herbal wreaths. I noticed that whenever it came time for them to put the

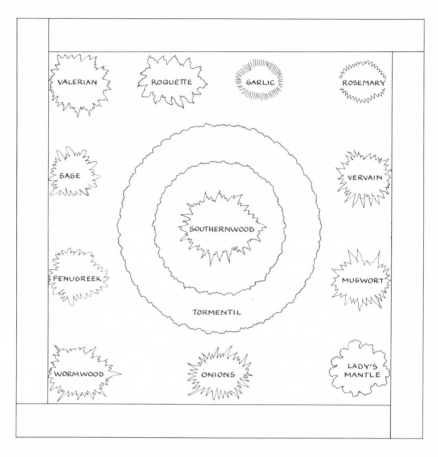

aromatic sprigs of rosemary into the wreaths, they would start giggling and would make bawdy jokes.

Ginseng, often touted for its aphrodisiac qualities, is not included in this plan because it will not grow well in a sunny area. For some reason, word about ginseng has spread to teenage boys— every spring I make many sales of ginseng plants to youngsters who clearly are not gardeners.

GARLIC	P	24″	Bulb
LADY'S MANTLE	P	12″	4
ONIONS	B	18″	Bulb
ROQUETTE	A	10″	3
*ROSEMARY	[TP]	4′	5
*SAGE	P	24″	5
SOUTHERNWOOD	P	3′	4
TORMENTIL	P	6″	3/4
VALERIAN	P	3′	4
VERVAIN	P	24″	2
WORMWOOD	P	24″	2/4

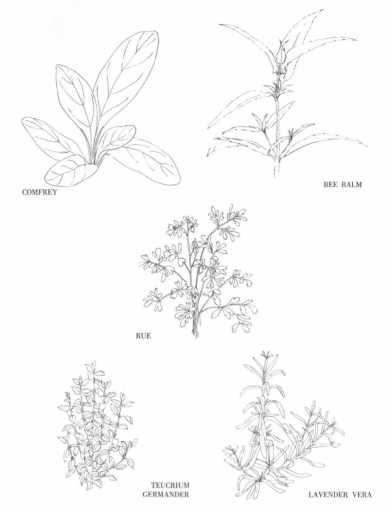

COMFREY

BEE BALM

RUE

TEUCRIUM
GERMANDER

LAVENDER VERA

COLONIAL GARDEN

These are the herbs that were most commonly included in 18th-century kitchen gardens and that served the housewives in those days for their everyday culinary, medicinal and dyeing needs. The herbs in the center have been planted within the spokes of an old wagon wheel.

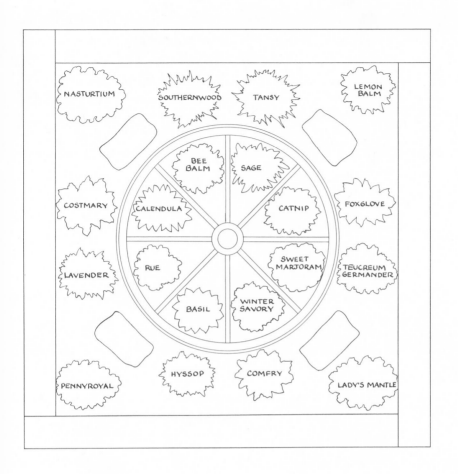

*BASIL	A	18″	2
BEE BALM	P	30″	4
CALENDULA	A	24″	2/3
CATNIP	P	18″	1/4
COMFREY	P	36″	4
COSTMARY	P	36″	4
FOXGLOVE	B	36″	2
HYSSOP	P	24″	2
LADY'S MANTLE	P	12″	4
LAVENDER VERA	P	18″	2/5
LEMON BALM	P	18″	4/2
*MARJORAM	TP	12″	1
NASTURTIUM	A	8″	3

PENNYROYAL MINT	P	3″	3
RUE	P	24″	2
*SAGE	P	24″	5
SOUTHERNWOOD	P	3′	4
TANSY	P	36″	4
TEUCRIUM			
GERMANDER	P	15″	5
WINTER SAVORY	P	12″	2

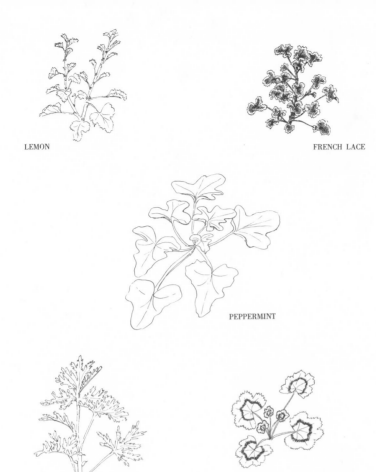

LEMON

FRENCH LACE

PEPPERMINT

ROSE

COCONUT

SCENTED GERANIUM GARDEN

This is an increasingly popular type of garden because there are so many scented geraniums to pick from—about 200 varieties with a wide range of leaf patterns, growing habits and rose, fruit or spice aromas—and because they make excellent house plants and so can be brought indoors for the winter in northern areas. Like the mints, thymes and sages, they are a natural collector's item.

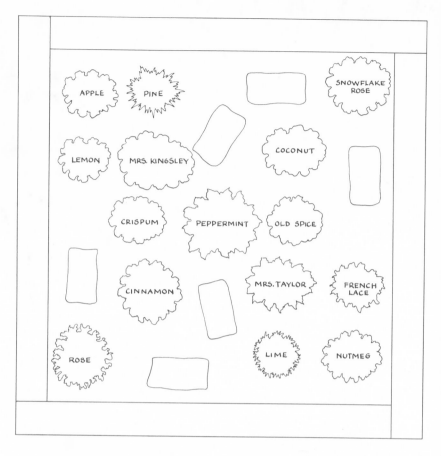

They're tough to start from seed. Seed is available, but it's expensive and sometimes does not come out true to the type on the label even if you do succeed in getting it to sprout. An alternative in collecting rare varieties is to order them as young plants through the mail. If you do this, buy from suppliers no more than two or three shipping days away, or have them shipped by air. Otherwise the plants are likely to perish in transit.

If you can't buy young plants close to home, the next best way to propagate is by taking cuttings off a friend's established plants in spring for development in a bright window. They are harder to start from cuttings than their cousins, the familiar bright-flowering geraniums, because they are highly susceptible to rotting. Therefore, be sure to use a well-drained sand/perlite root-ing medium and to water conservatively during the four weeks that most cuttings will require before rooting. Be especially care-ful not to get the cuttings wet on cloudy days. Select sprigs that are tender—neither too soft nor too woody. Once rooted, trans-plant into standard planting medium in 4-inch pots and sink in garden (after danger of frost is past).

The garden plan here includes large growing types, such as the peppermint geranium, and compact growers like French lace. It reflects the three main types of scents—rose (of which there are over fifty varieties), fruit and spice. And it has a sampling of the main various growing styles—the upright such as lemon crispum, the trailing, such as the coconut, and the bushy, such as nutmeg or pine.

Smaller-growing scented geraniums may be brought inside at the end of the growing season by digging them up, potting them and trimming any larger, more unruly branches. If they have been kept trimmed throughout the summer (leaves can be used for making jams and jellies or potpourris, or floating on your bath water), most will remain small enough to be brought inside with-out too much fuss. Unlike almost all the other herbs, scented gera-niums do not require a window with a full sunny southern exposure. They do well in any window with as little as four hours' sun. They'll remain semi-dormant until early March when they'll begin to put on new growth again.

For convenience, and also to spare your plant unnecessary root damage, you can plant your smaller geraniums in 6 to 8 inch pots when you first set them out into the garden in the spring.

Larger growing varieties—in this plan, the rose, snowflake

and peppermint—simply get too big in the garden to bring indoors intact. If you want any of them for company over the winter, start them from cuttings taken off the established plant in late summer.

APPLE	[A]	12″	5
CINNAMON	[A]	18″	5
COCONUT	[A]	15″	5
FRENCH LACE	[A]	18″	5
LEMON	[A]	24″	5
LEMON CRISPUM	[A]	24″	5
LIME	[A]	18″	5
MRS. KINGSLEY	[A]	24″	5
MRS. TAYLOR	[A]	24″	5
NUTMEG	[A]	18″	5
OLD SPICE	[A]	18″	5
PEPPERMINT	A	24″	5
PINE	[A]	18″	5
ROSE	A	24″	5
SNOWFLAKE	A	24″	5

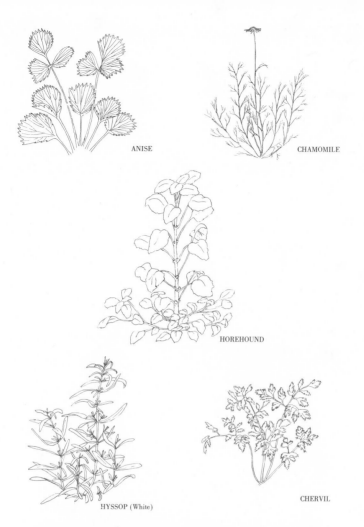

ANISE

CHAMOMILE

HOREHOUND

HYSSOP (White)

CHERVIL

WHITE-FLOWERING HERBS

In this and the three succeeding plans, the herbs were selected primarily for the colors of their blossoms, and were separated, the whites from the blues, and the blues from the reds, and the reds from the yellows, for a couple of reasons.

First, it provides an easy reference for gardeners interested in quickly finding out what herbs produce what color blooms.

Also, it makes sense botanically to keep some herb families

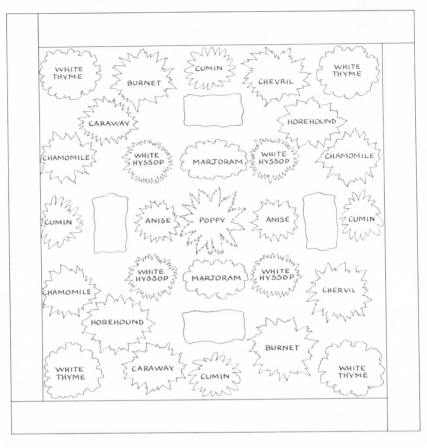

separated by color. If you tried to grow all three shades of hyssop together, for example, cross-pollination would eventually spoil your effort, and you might end up with only one faded color.

Most of the perennial herbs will not reach blossoming stage until the second year. Some perennials will flower the first year in regions with longer growing seasons if transplanted into the garden early enough in spring.

In any case, none of the perennials stays in flower for more than two or three weeks. They should be cut back as soon as the blooms are finished to foster new growth and a possible second flowering.

Of course, if you're cutting stems and leaves continuously for other uses, you won't see any flowers. If you make pizza every week, you may never see the beautiful pale purplish-pink blossoms that the oregano plant will give you when it is allowed to fully develop.

Two pretty white-flowering herbs are not included in this first plan: angelica because it gets too large for a garden this size, and sweet woodruff because it belongs in a shady spot.

ANISE	A	24″	3
BURNET	P	18″	2
CHAMOMILE	A	18″	2
CARAWAY	B	24″	2
*CHERVIL	A	24″	2
CUMIN	A	8″	2
HOREHOUND	P	18″	2
HYSSOP (White)	P	24″	2
*MARJORAM	TP	12″	1
POPPY	A	36″	2
WHITE-FLOWERING THYME	P	1″	4

ORDER OF FLOWERING

First Year:	*Subsequent Years:*
chamomile	caraway
thyme	burnet
chervil	poppy
anise	chamomile
cumin	chervil
marjoram (possibly)	thyme
hyssop (possibly)	marjoram
	horehound
	hyssop
	anise
	cumin

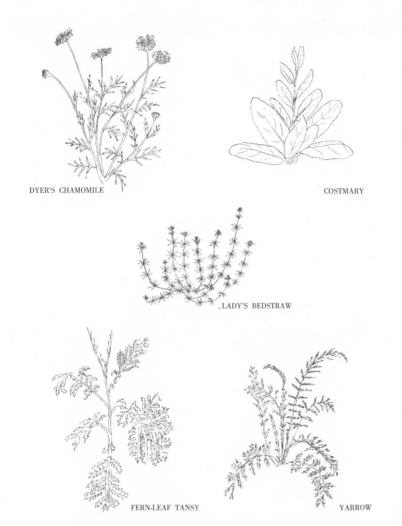

DYER'S CHAMOMILE

COSTMARY

LADY'S BEDSTRAW

FERN-LEAF TANSY

YARROW

YELLOW & ORANGE
FLOWERING GARDEN

This garden is as good a cutting garden as any, and beginning in July you can regularly bring in bunches of various daisy-shaped flowers. It is the boldest, tallest-growing and potentially most productive of all the flowering-herb gardens.

Caraway, mustard, fennel and a few of the common culinary herbs will also flower yellow when let go to seed, but they are not

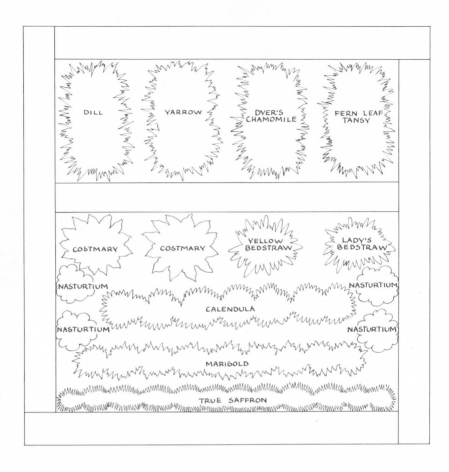

included here because their blooms are nothing special.

Dill is included because its umbrella-shaped flower is so attractive and works so effectively in bouquets or dried arrangements.

CALENDULA	A	24″	2/3
COSTMARY	P	36″	4
*DILL	A	30″	3
DYER'S CHAMOMILE	P	30″	2
FERN-LEAF TANSY	P	24″	4
LADY'S BEDSTRAW	P	24″	2
MARIGOLDS	A	15″	2
NASTURTIUM	A	8″	3
SAFFRON	P	8″	Bulb
YARROW	P	24″	2/4

ORDER OF FLOWERING

First Year:	*Subsequent Years:*
marigold	marigold
calendula	yarrow
nasturtium	calendula
dill	nasturtium
tansy	yellow chamomile
saffron	lady's bedstraw
	costmary
	dill
	tansy
	saffron

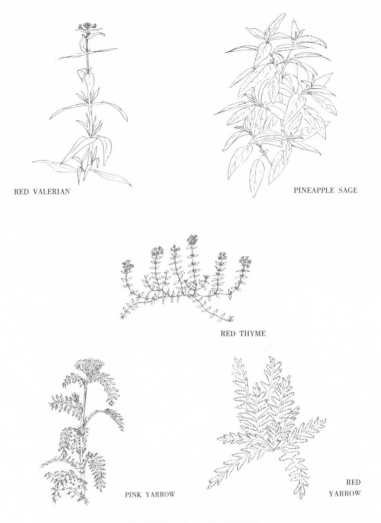

RED VALERIAN   PINEAPPLE SAGE

RED THYME

PINK YARROW   RED YARROW

PINK & RED FLOWERING HERBS

Except for the pineapple sage, all these herbs are hardy perennials. As with the preceding flower plans, they could be equally well planted in border areas or as cutting gardens in the yard.

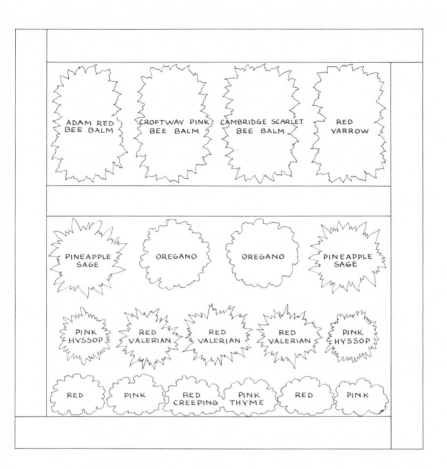

BEE BALM	P	30"	4
*OREGANO	P	24"	4
PINEAPPLE SAGE	TP	30"	5
PINK HYSSOP	P	24"	2
PINK THYME	P	3"	4
RED THYME	P	3"	4
RED VALERIAN	P	3'	4
YARROW	P	24"	2/4

ORDER OF FLOWERING

First Year:	*Subsequent Years:*
thymes	thymes
bee balm	bee balm
pineapple sage	hyssop
hyssop	oregano
oregano	pineapple sage
red valerian	yarrow
yarrow	red valerian

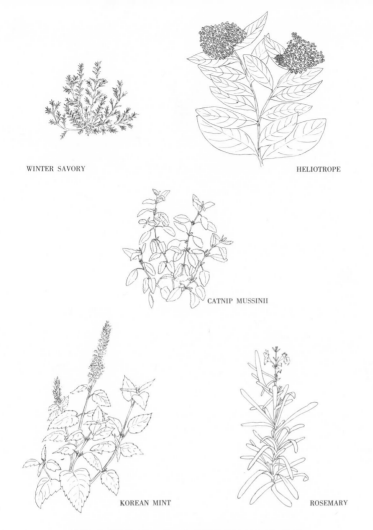

WINTER SAVORY

HELIOTROPE

CATNIP MUSSINII

KOREAN MINT

ROSEMARY

BLUE & PURPLE
FLOWERING HERBS

With the exception of borage and heliotrope, all the herbs in this garden of subtle, rather than dramatic, blue- and purple-flowering herbs, are perennials.

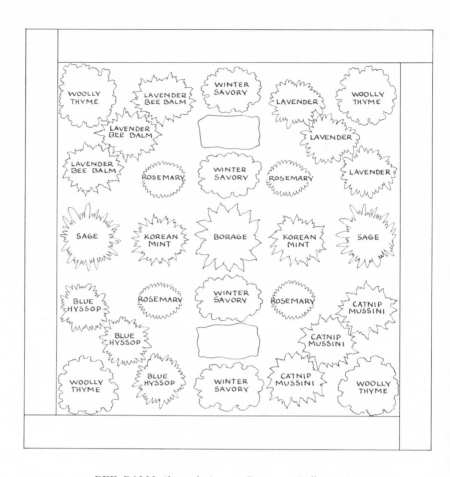

BEE BALM (lavender)	P	30"	4
BORAGE	A	30"	2
CATNIP MUSSINII	P	18"	4
HELIOTROPE	[A]	18"	5/2
HYSSOP (blue)	P	24"	2
KOREAN MINT	P	30"	2
LAVENDER VERA	P	18"	2/5
*ROSEMARY	[TP]	4'	5
*SAGE	P	24"	5
WINTER SAVORY	P	12"	2
WOOLLY THYME	P	1"	4

ORDER OF FLOWERING

First Year:	*Subsequent Years:*
borage	borage
heliotrope	heliotrope
thyme	woolly thyme
catnip	winter savory
Korean mint	hyssop
	catnip
	bee balm
	rosemary
	lavender
	sage
	Korean mint

182

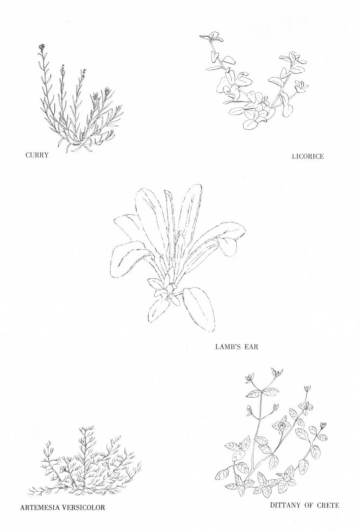

CURRY

LICORICE

LAMB'S EAR

ARTEMESIA VERSICOLOR

DITTANY OF CRETE

SILVER GARDEN

This garden creates an exquisite effect in midsummer. The sun brings out the subtle variations in gray and silver in the plants, and also the delicate differences in the various leaf shapes and growing patterns. It doesn't require a great deal of attention— certainly nowhere near the time and effort required by the basic

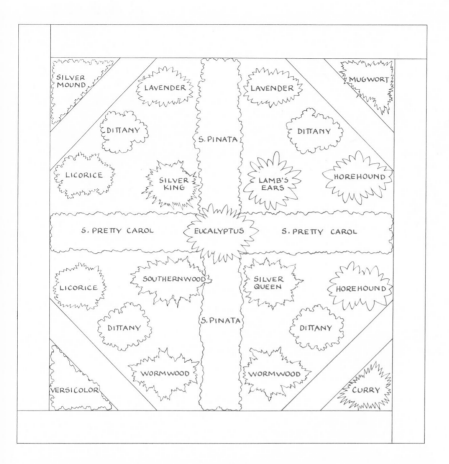

Within the diagram:

SILVER MOUND · LAVENDER · LAVENDER · MUGWORT
DITTANY · S. PINATA · DITTANY
LICORICE · SILVER KING · LAMB'S EARS · HOREHOUND
S. PRETTY CAROL · EUCALYPTUS · S. PRETTY CAROL
LICORICE · SOUTHERNWOOD · SILVER QUEEN · HOREHOUND
DITTANY · S. PINATA · DITTANY
VERSICOLOR · WORMWOOD · WORMWOOD · CURRY

culinary garden—yet results can be stunning. The plants can be cut in fall and saved for use in dried arrangements in winter.

During wet weather, the artemesias—silver king, silver queen and silver mound—are fungus-prone. If rotting develops, cut away bad parts of the plants affected to promote new, healthy growth.

ARTEMESIAS:

ROMAN WORMWOOD	P	18″	4
SILVER KING	P	24″	4
SILVER MOUND	P	6″	4
SILVER QUEEN	P	24″	4
VERSICOLOR	P	15″	4/5
CURRY	P	15″	5

DITTANY OF CRETE	[A]	10"	5
EUCALYPTUS	[TP]	6'	2
HOREHOUND	P	18"	2
LAMB'S EAR	P	12"	4
LAVENDER VERA	P	18"	2/5
LICORICE	[A]	12"	5
MUGWORT	P	3'	2/4
PINNATA SANTOLINA	[P]	12"	5
PRETTY CAROL			
SANTOLINA	[TP]	12"	5
SOUTHERNWOOD	P	3'	4

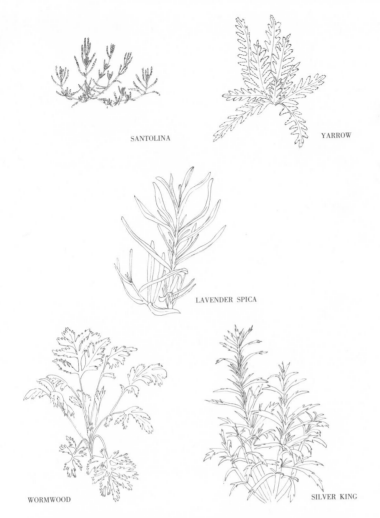

SANTOLINA

YARROW

LAVENDER SPICA

WORMWOOD

SILVER KING

CHRISTMAS WREATH GARDEN

Like the clock-shaped thyme garden, this garden takes several years to develop fully in the yard—but it may be used as a source of material for a home-made herbal Christmas wreath beginning in the first year.

Most of the space in the garden is devoted to the santolina. That's because I think it's the best prime herb material for wreath-making. Artemesias can be planted and used in this quantity in-

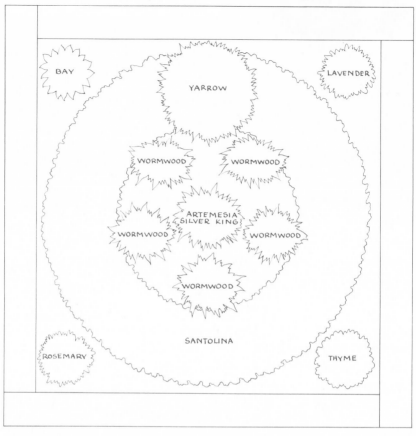

stead, but they have a tendency to get too brittle to work with easily. Statice is another common base material for wreaths. It's easy to work with, but it is not an attractive grower in small gardens—it gets too weedy, so I've left it out altogether.

How to Make an Herbal Wreath

Harvest the yarrow in late summer, after it has flowered, bringing it indoors and hanging it to dry until the rest of the materials are ready. This should be in late fall—about the time you bring the tender bay and rosemary indoors in their pots to make sure the frost doesn't get them.

For the wreath form, buy a steel ring from a local hobby shop, crafts store or florist. It will cost fifty cents or so, and will give you a much more solid base to work on than one home-made from coat hangers. Also, buy a spool of fine (22 to 26 gauge) green florist wire and a couple of dozen 3-inch florist's wire picks.

Step One: Wrap the metal ring with wormwood, using the wire to hold this feathery herb in place, until it is about three to four inches thick.

Step Two: Cut up the santolina into 6-inch long stems. Place fan-shaped bunches of three to four stems directly upon the wormwood (with the form laying flat on your work table), then secure the stems with wire. Take the next fan-shaped bunch of santolina and place it so that the bushier end covers the stem end of the first bunch. Keep adding santolina bunches in this way. When you reach the end of the circle, lift up your first bunch and slip the stems of your last bunch under it.

Step Three: Select specimen flower-heads of the yarrow, bay, thyme, lavender and rosemary and attach to florist picks, then insert into the wreath as you wish, making sure each selection is secured in the wormwood base and that the herb you're displaying doesn't get buried in the layer of santolina.

Step Four: Embellish, if you wish, with red chile or cayenne peppers, garlic or shallot bulbs, cinnamon sticks, nutmegs, bitter-sweet, etc.

(Note: If in making the wreath you notice that your herbs have become too dry or brittle, mist or sprinkle them with luke-warm water.)

*BAY	[TP]	2–6'	5
COMMON SILVER THYME	[P]	8"	5
LAVENDER SPICA	P	24"	2/5
*ROSEMARY	[TP]	4'	5
GRAY SANTOLINA	P	12"	5
SILVER KING	P	24"	4
WORMWOOD	P	24"	2/4
YARROW	P	24"	2/4

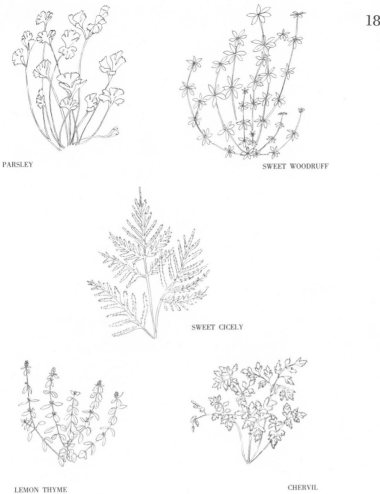

PARSLEY

SWEET WOODRUFF

SWEET CICELY

LEMON THYME

CHERVIL

SHADY GARDEN

This plan is for areas that get less than four hours of sun a day
and is popular with people who have a lot of trees to contend with.
It will not work in dense shade where only mushrooms grow, however. Some of the herbs included here—parsley, tarragon, cress
and salad burnet—also do well in full sun. The others perform
their best in less than full sunlight.

Ginseng and goldenseal are two shade-loving herbs *not in-*

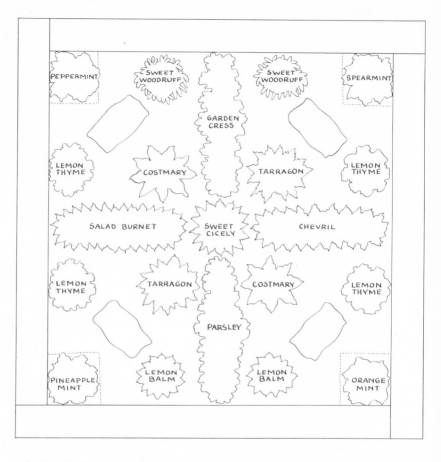

cluded in this plan because they require unusual soil conditions. They do best in a sloping natural woodland setting where there's lots of drainage and yet plenty of leaf mold in the ground.

Angelica, a biennial that does well in shade, isn't included also because it grows to such a large size that by the second year it would overwhelm this small area.

BURNET	P	18″	2
*CHERVIL	A	24″	2
COSTMARY	P	36″	4
CRESS	A	6″	3
LEMON BALM	P	18″	4/2

MINTS:

ORANGE	P	24″	4
PEPPERMINT	P	24″	4
PINEAPPLE	P	12″	4
*SPEARMINT	P	18″	4
*PARSLEY	B	8″	3
*TARRAGON	P	30″	4
LEMON THYME	P	4″	4
SWEET CICELY	P	3′	4
SWEET WOODRUFF	P	12″	4/5

PART IV

Herb Culture Guide

HERBS MENTIONED in this book and used in the garden plans are indexed here alphabetically by popular name, along with details on the propagation and cultural techniques that may be special to each plant.

The line of "vital statistics" for each herb is similar to that used throughout the plans section. It consists of these elements:

AMBROSIA   Popular Name
A   Life Cycle
18″   Average Height
2/3   Way to Propagate
Chenopodium   Botanical Name

First element: *popular name* of herb (Asterisk (*) appears if herb is one of the basic fifteen culinaries.)

Second element: *life cycle*

A   annual
B   biennial
P   perennial
TP   tender perennial

Note: if life cycle code is bracketed, such as [A], [P], or [TP], herb described may be brought in from the garden and kept as a house plant in a sunny window during the winter.

Third element: *average height* of plant at maturity under normal growing conditions.

Fourth element: *propagation method* suggested for each herb according to the five methods discussed in the main text:

Group 1   cluster sowing indoors
Group 2   spot sowing indoors
Group 3   cluster sowing outdoors
Group 4   making root divisions
Group 5   taking stem cuttings.

The *bulb method* of propagation is also included to cover some plants. As mentioned earlier, the methods recommended are not necessarily the only ways to propagate the herbs in question. But generally they are the easiest or most practical, considering such factors as seed germination rate or availability of existing plants.

Fifth element: the official Latin or *botanical name* for each herb. Whenever possible, these names conform to Bailey's *Hortus Third* (Macmillan, 1976), the definitive source of horticultural data for botanists and plantsmen, compiled by L. H. Bailey Hortorium, Cornell University.

AMBROSIA   A   18″   2/3   *Chenopodium Botrys*
Also called JERUSALEM OAK
Easily started from seed. Self-sows every year, but not so prolifically as to become a nuisance.

ANGELICA   B   6′   3   *Angelica Archangelica*
Seeds must be really fresh to germinate, so I don't recommend buying them in the spring. Instead, locate fresh seed in fall and sow immediately outdoors. Seedlings will emerge, then die down to the ground after freezing, and reappear next spring as strong healthy plants. Unlike most herbs, this large grower likes a rich soil. It also does better when it gets shade half the day. Will self-sow.

ANISE   A   24″   3   *Pimpinella Anisum*
Easily started from seed but doesn't like being transplanted because of tap root. Sow at shallow depth in spot you want plants to grow. Mound plants as they develop, as stems tend to be weak. Both seed and leaves have licorice flavor. Harvest flower clusters when seeds turn brown.

ARTEMISIA VERSICOLOR   P   15″   4/5   *Artemisia versicolor*
One of the few herbs actually called by its Latin name. Must be started from root division or cutting in spring. Don't mulch, as it rots quite easily. Subdivide after third growing season.
See also SILVER MOUND, SILVER KING, SILVER QUEEN, TARRAGON, ROMAN WORMWOOD, WORMWOOD.

BALM. See BEE BALM, LEMON BALM.

BASILS

*BASIL   A   18″   2   *Ocimum Basilicum*
Also called BUSH BASIL, SWEET BASIL.

DWARF BASIL   A   12″   2   *Ocimum Minimum*
Shortest of basils with smallest leaf. True seeds hard to find. Many seed
companies give you bush basil instead.

FINE-LEAF BASIL   A   15″   2   *Ocimum Basilicum feinum*
Good border plant. Medium size leaf and plant.

INDIAN BASIL   A   24″   2   *Ocimum Gratissimum*
Seeds hard to come by. Herbs used in India in medicinal applications.

LEMON BASIL   A   15″   2   *Ocimum Citriodorum*
Distinct lemon flavor.

LETTUCE-LEAF BASIL A   18″   2   *Ocimum Basilicum crispum*
Largest leaves of all the basils; seed readily available.

PURPLE BASIL   A   18″   2   *Ocimum Basilicum purpurea*
Also called DARK OPAL BASIL.
Cross-pollination with other basils will develop seed that produces plants
streaked with green, so make sure of the reliability of your seed source
for this one.

SACRED BASIL   A   30″   2   *Ocimum sanctum*
Largest of all the basils. Should be hilled or staked. Seeds hard to come by.

*BAY   [TP]   2′–6′   5   *Laurus nobilis*

BEDSTRAW. See LADY'S BEDSTRAW.

BEE BALMS   P   30″   4   *Monarda didyma varieties*
Also called BERGAMOT, OSWEGO TEA.
Start from division in early spring as soon as new growth appears. If you
wait until it reaches 8 inches, you'll risk losing the plant in dividing. Erect

grower and rapid spreader, it should be divided yearly after second season as root systems become highly developed. Scarlet, lavender, pink and white varieties also available.

BORAGE   A   30″   2   *Borago officinalis*
Simple to start from seed—if seed is fresh. Germination rate is practically 100 percent. Likes a richer soil than most herbs. Supposed to self-sow, too, but I've never seen it happen in any of my gardens. Blue flowers, hairy leaves.

BURDOCK   B   36″   3   *Arctium minus*
Quick grower, large leaves, deep tap root. Produces burrs midseason in second year. Best to cut flowers so that seed does not scatter, as this herb resows easily and could become a pest. Not to be confused with the larger-growing edible herb favored in Japanese cooking, called gobo (*Arctium lappa*).

BURNET   P   18″   2   *Sanguisorba minor*
Also called SALAD BURNET.
For constant supply of cucumber-flavored greens for salads, keep cutting young leaves when four to five inches high. Divide after second growing season.

CALENDULA   A   24″   2/3   *Calendula officinalis*
Germinates in ten days at 65°. If started indoors, use peat pots. Keep picking the flowers and you'll get blooms all summer long.

CHAMOMILE   A   18″   2   *Matricaria Chamomilla*
Also called GERMAN CHAMOMILE.
Easily started from seed but does not transplant well unless very young. Sow in peat pots. Keep picking flowers for your teas before seed ripens or it will self-sow all over the garden.

DYER'S CHAMOMILE　　　P　　　30″　　　2　　　*Anthemis tinctoria*
Also called YELLOW CHAMOMILE.
Largest of all the chamomiles, produces a bright yellow daisy-type flower. Germinates easily, but seeds are harder to come by than other chamomiles. Divide after second growing season.

ROMAN CHAMOMILE　　　P　　　6″　　　1　　　*Anthemis nobilis*
Also called ENGLISH CHAMOMILE.
A terrific groundcover that will take all kinds of abuse and still come back. Does not bloom nearly as profusely as the tea chamomile.

CARAWAY　　　B　　　24″　　　2　　　*Carum Carvi*
Very hardy biennial which can be harvested for its seed early in second year. Young carrotlike seedlings do not transplant well, so start in peat pots which can be transplanted intact into garden. Sow outdoors (Group 3 method) in early fall to get crop of seed toward end of following growing season.

CATNIP　　　P　　　18″　　　1/4　　　*Nepeta Cataria*
Easily grown indoors from its tiny seeds; germinates in four days. Outdoor sowing must await warmer soil. Divide after second season. Self-sows readily so keep it from going to seed unless you have a lot of cats to support.

CATNIP MUSSINII　　　P　　　18″　　　4　　　*Nepeta Mussinii*
Much smaller than common catnip, with attractive silver-blue foliage. Not as delectable to cats, but excellent in dried bouquets. Hard to find the seed, so make a division in a friend's garden in early spring. Divide after second or third year.

CAYENNE PEPPER　　　A　　　30″　　　2　　　*Capsicum annuum*
Like all other peppers, this is relatively easy to grow from seed, but don't over-water young seedlings that are started indoors as they easily dampen off. Transplant into garden after all danger of frost is past. Needs mod-

erately rich soil. If you let a fruit or two fall to the ground during the growing season, the plant may self-sow.

*CHERVIL　　　A　　　24″　　　2　　　*Anthriscus Cerefolium*

CHIVES

*CHIVES　　　P　　　12″　　　1　　　*Allium Schoenoprasum*

CURLY CHIVES　　P　　6″　　4　　　*Allium senescens glaucum*
Shortest and slowest spreader of all the chive family. Produces blue-green foliage with striking lavender blossoms in July. Seeds hard to find, so buy established plants or divide a neighbor's cluster in the spring. Does better in soil that has been well-limed.

GARLIC CHIVES　　　P　　　12″　　　4　　　*Allium tuberosum*
Also called BROAD-LEAFED CHIVES.
Try planting in rows around vegetable garden to deter pests. Dig up and divide every fall. Lovely white blossoms appear in July.

GIGANTIUM CHIVES　　P　　36″　　Bulb　　*Allium giganteum*
Plant the four-inch-wide bulb in fall (when available along with Holland bulbs at larger garden centers). Bury eight to twelve inches, preferably in corners of garden where it won't get in the way. Large, broad silver-blue leaves appear in early spring, followed by thick stalk in center of plant, which produces a high, eight-inch-round lavender blossom in July. Will reappear every year if bulb not destroyed. Does better in well-limed soil.

MOLLY CHIVES　　　P　　　15″　　Bulb　　*Allium Moly*
Plant tiny bulbs in fall, three inches deep at six-inch intervals. Produces yellow blooms in late May.

ROSEUM CHIVES　　P　　12″　　Bulb　　*Allium roseum*
Plant same as molly. Roseum produces rose-colored blossoms, slightly

larger than molly's, in early June.

COLTSFOOT   P   12"   3/4   *Tussilago Farfara*
Grows easily from seed, but the seed is hard to obtain, so best to make
root division in very early spring. If from seed, orange flower blooms in
early spring of second growing season before broad, hoof-shaped leaves
appear. Cart before horse—a botanical oddity.

COMFREY   P   36"   4   *Symphytum officinale*
Easily started from root divisions in early spring. Extremely hardy, will
spread rapidly in any sunny location. Divide yearly to keep it confined. Leaves most highly valued for their healing qualities and protein
content.

*CORIANDER   A   24"   2   *Coriandrum sativum*

CORN-SALAD   A   8"   3   *Valerianella Locusta*
Grows quickly from seed if soil is warm. Ready in forty-five days; sow
successively for continuous harvest all summer.

COSTMARY   P   36"   4   *Chrysanthemum Balsamita*
Also called BIBLE LEAF.
Seeds hard to locate, but divides easily in early spring. Will grow well
in shade, but will not blossom unless in sun. Divide after second growing
season as it becomes too large and straggly. Got nickname from use as
bookmark in Bibles in earlier times. Versatile herb—can be used in teas,
potpourris and salads.

CRESS   A   6"   3   *Lepidium sativum*
Also called GARDEN CRESS.
Not to be confused with water cress. Grows quickly from seed, does better
in moderately rich soil. Make several sowings during summer. Upland
cress variety has the neatest, most compact growing pattern.

CUMIN   A   8″   2   *Cuminum Cyminum*
Takes 100 days to fully mature and needs warm weather, so must be started indoors up north. Needs richer soil than the average herb. Its weak stems make it tend to grow floppy. The desired seed is formed in attractive white blossoms.

CURRY   [P]   15″   5   *Helichrysum angustifolium*
Not to be confused with curry powder, which is a combination of several ground spices. Can be started only from cuttings. Can be brought indoors in winter as its silver foliage makes it an attractive house plant. Supposed to be tender, but it has survived four straight winters in our Connecticut gardens. Leaves have the curry flavor.

DANDELION   P   4″   3   *Taraxacum officinale*
Simple to start from seed sown sparingly. Keep picking flowers to promote leafy growth and also to prevent it spreading into your lawn areas.

*DILL   A   30″   3   *Anethum graveolens*

DILL BOUQUET   A   24″   3   *Anethum graveolens var.*
Seeds are hard to find, but in some ways this variety is more desirable in garden than standard dill because of short, compact growing pattern. Re-sows itself readily so is often called a "perennial."

DITTANY OF CRETE   [A]   10″   5   *Origanum Dictamnus*
Easy to start from cuttings unless it is overwatered. Its root system does better bound in a small pot. Will survive as a house plant if trimmed and brought indoors in clay pot to a sunny window in winter months. Replant in garden in following spring.

DYER'S BROOM   P   18″   2   *Genista tinctoria*
Divide after second growing season. If allowed to go to seed, will self-sow freely.

ELECAMPANE   P   4'   4   *Inula Helenium*
Seeds are hard to find and hard to germinate, so start from division of a
friend's established plant in early spring. Because of its height and broad
leaves, this plant requires more moisture than most herbs do.

EUCALYPTUS   [TP]   6'   2   *Eucalyptus Globulus*
A tree that grows to 100 feet in its native habitat, this makes an excellent
tub plant up north if you can keep it in a sunny window indoors in the
winter. Needs a moderately rich soil.

FENNEL   A   30"   3   *Foeniculum vulgare*
Treat exactly like dill.

FENUGREEK   A   18"   3   *Trigonella Foenum—graecum*
Sometimes confused with fennel because name is similar. Grows like sweet
clover, needs a bit more fertilization than average herb does, and extra
dry conditions. Seed pods resemble string beans.

FOXGLOVE   B   36"   2   *Digitalis purpurea*
Seeds are very slow to germinate. Beware of overwatering young seedlings.
Transplant to a rich, well-drained soil. Full sun is essential for develop-
ment of the digitalis content in leaves. Flowers second year.

GARDEN CRESS. See CRESS.

GARLIC   P   24"   Bulb   *Allium sativum*
Plant cloves of this flat-leaved onion in fall four inches deep. Harvest in
late summer after leaves have dried and died down. Save some for re-
planting in fall for next year's crop.

GERANIUMS. See SCENTED GERANIUMS.

GINSENG   P   24"   2/roots   *Panax quinquefolius*
Very hard to grow from seed. Buy established three-year-old roots instead.

Needs a well-drained, rich, loamy soil in a cool, shady spot.

GOLDENSEAL   P   12"   2/roots   *Hydrastis canadensis*
Treat exactly as ginseng.

HELIOTROPE   [A]   18"   5/2   *Heliotropium arborescens*
Relatively easy to start from seed indoors, but a better growth pattern
develops when cuttings are made from choice plants. Prefers moderately
rich soil. Will survive as a house plant if trimmed and brought indoors
in clay pot to a sunny window in winter.

HOREHOUND   P   18"   2   *Marrubium vulgare*
Easily started from seed; germinates in ten days at 70 degrees, twenty
days at 55 degrees. Will grow in partial shade, but prefers full sun. Will
rot away in wet locations. Though hardy, it will not survive a wet winter.
Divide after second growing season.

HORSERADISH   P   24"   4   *Armoracia lapathifolia rusticana*
Start from a root or piece thereof in very early spring for a good fall crop.
Grows tenaciously in any kind of soil in a sunny location.

HYSSOPS   P   24"   2   *Hyssopus officinalis varieties*
All the flowering hyssops are easy to grow from seed, and if the seed is
fresh you'll get 90 per cent germination. Prefers a well-limed soil and will
do fairly well in partial shade. Natural deterrent of white fly in gardens and
greenhouses. Old plants become very woody so divide every two years.
Replace with fresh plants when too woody and unattractive.

JERUSALEM ARTICHOKE   P   7'   *Helianthus tuberosus*
Start from tubers in early spring. Grows quite tall and produces a daisy
flower in late fall.

LADY'S BEDSTRAW   P   24"   2   *Galium verum*
Also called YELLOW BEDSTRAW.
Seeds germinate slowly and not very well, but once established in garden, the plants spread well and should be divided every spring beginning with the third growing season. Does well in partial shade.

LADY'S MANTLE   P   12"   4   *Alchemilla vulgaris*
Best way to propagate is by division in early spring, but requires more careful handling than most perennials because of its deep tap roots. If allowed to go to seed, it will sometimes resow itself in early fall; transplant these seedlings to a cold frame for distribution to friends and neighbors next spring. Susceptible to rot unless in a well-drained spot.

LAMB'S EAR   P   12"   4   *Stachys lanata*
Also called BETONY.
Divide in early spring and give it plenty of room. To keep it from overcrowding itself, redivide every second year.

LARKSPUR   A   30"   2   *Delphinium Consolida*
Harvest flowers when they appear in order to get second blooming. If allowed to go to seed, plant will self-sow, but new seedlings won't usually reach flowering stage before frost in northern areas.

LAVENDER MUNSTEAD P 15" 2/5 *Lavendula angustifolia Munstead*

LAVENDER SPICA   P   24"   2/5   *Lavandula Spica*
Also called ENGLISH LAVENDER.

LAVENDER VERA   P   18"   2/5   *Lavandula officinalis*
All laboriously started from seed indoors, so I prefer to propagate via cuttings because I get more uniform and compact growth from the new plants. Take a deep breath and trim plants the first year to keep them from flowering and so promote bushier growth, and a prolific harvest the next year. Thereafter, trim every year after flowers have been harvested. Lavenders

have long tap roots so are not easily transplanted after two years. Munstead has smallest leaves and is most compact grower. Spica is largest but least hardy—often weather kills in severe winter. Vera is best choice for most gardeners.

LEEKS   P   24″   1   *Allium Porrum*
Start indoors from seed about sixty days before putting them in garden; separate seedlings and transplant six to eight inches apart.

LEMON BALM   P   18″   4/2   *Melissa officinalis*
Easily started from division or seed in early spring. Does well in full sun or semi-shade. Harvest several times. Divide every year after second year as it spreads quickly.

LEMON VERBENA   [A]   6′   5   *Aloysia triphylla*
Has the truest lemon scent of all the lemon-flavored herbs, so extremely popular ingredient in beverages and potpourris. Needs a rich soil and lots of sun and warmth. Start from cuttings if you can't buy established plants, but be patient as it is one of the hardest herbs to propagate. As house plant over winter, needs tub-sized planter and sunny window. Goes into semi-dormancy until February, then starts to produce new leafy growth. Used to be classified *Lippia citriodora*.

LICORICE   [A]   12″   5   *Helichrysum petiolatum*
A decorative herb, not the true licorice plant, with attractive silver-gray foliage that makes for an excellent house plant in pots or hanging baskets.

LOVAGE   P   6′   2   *Levisticum officinale*
Start from seed indoors about six weeks before you intend to set it in garden—no earlier or its rapid growth will cause problems. Needs richer soil and more moisture than most herbs because of its size. Will tolerate partial shade. Divide every other year in early spring unless you happen to have plenty of room for it in the garden.

MADDER   P   12″   4   *Rubica tinctorum*
Seeds are hard to obtain so find a friend with madder and make a division
in early spring—there'll be plenty of underground runners to pick from.
Divide every year after second growing season to keep confined.

MARIGOLDS   A   15″   2   *Tagetes patula*
Probably the easiest of all annual herbs to start from seed. Thanks to extensive hybridization, now comes in more sizes than poodles. Shorter ones
work best in limited areas, though.

*MARJORAM   TP   12″   1   *Origanum Majorana*
Also called SWEET MARJORAM.

WILD MARJORAM   P   18″   1   *Origanum vulgare*
Hardier than its sweet cousin. Divide after second growing season to keep
confined. Self-sows profusely if allowed to drop seed.

MINTS

APPLE MINT   P   24″   4   *Mentha rotundifolia*
Grows taller but not as profusely as the other mints, with larger, woolier
leaves.

BERGAMOT MINT   P   18″   4   *Mentha aquatica crispa*
Lemon flavored, frequently used (along with apple, pineapple and orange
mints) in iced drinks and fruit salads. Not to be confused with bee balm,
which is sometimes called bergamot.

CURLY MINT   P   24″   4   *Mentha spicata—Crispata*
Almost exactly like spearmint except crinkly.

GOLDEN MINT   P   18″   4   *Mentha spicata—variegata*
A variation on spearmint, bleeding yellow hue to leaves.

KOREAN MINT   P   30"   2   *Agastache rugosa*
Interesting but little-known tea herb, best started from seed simply because
it may be hard to find plants from which to make a division. Will grow up
to four feet tall in second year in a rich soil.

ORANGE MINT   P   24"   4   *Mentha citrata*
True orange tang.

PENNYROYAL MINT   P   3"   3   *Mentha Pulegium*
Short and small-leafed, but strongly flavored. Unlike most mints, this one is
easy to start from seed.

PEPPERMINT   P   24"   4   *Mentha piperita*
Second most popular of all the mints, behind spearmint; has darker stem.

PINEAPPLE MINT   P   12"   4   *Mentha rotundifolia variegata*
Attractive variegated leaf. Much smaller than its first cousin, apple mint.
When propagating, pick most desirable color variation in leaf.

*SPEARMINT   P   18"   4   *Mentha spicata*

MOTHERWORT   P   30"   2   *Leonurus Cardiaca*
Easy and quick from seed. Control by dividing regularly after second
growing season.

MUGWORT   P   3'   2/4   *Artemesia vulgaris*
The only artemesia for which seeds are readily available. Rapid grower,
very hardy, keep confined by dividing after second year.

MULLEIN   B   6'   2   *Verbascum Thapsus*
Easily started from seed—germinates in ten days at 70 degrees—and
transplanted into garden when young, but sets down deep tap root so is

hard to move after second year. Needs very dry, poor soil to do well. Fertilize and it practically shrinks. Produces huge velvety leaves at the base of its large flower spike. Cut the flower before seed ripens and drops, or you will have literally thousands of seedlings springing up in your garden next year.

MUSTARD   A   18″   3   *Brassica juncea*
Germinates in thirty hours at 70 degrees—that's fast. For plenty of tender young leaves, sow succession crops of this cabbage relative.

NASTURTIUM   A   8″   3   *Tropaeolum majus*
Easily started from seed outdoors, but make sure soil is warm.

NETTLE   P   36″   3   *Urtica dioica*
The herb least loved by my workers in the greenhouses. Easy to start from seed, but hard to transplant mainly because even as a seedling it has stinging spines. Keep dividing after second year in garden to confine growth.

ONIONS   B   18″   Bulb   *Allium Cepa*
Depending on variety selected, may be started from seed or sets (tiny bulbs). The latter are simpler and quicker. If sowing from seed, be sure to thin seedlings to four inches apart. Harvest in fall after stalks have turned brown and fallen over. Prefers sweet, moderately rich soil.

EGYPTIAN ONIONS   P   24″   Bulb   *Allium Cepa Viviparum*
Plant bulbs in fall. Tiny new bulblets develop in clusters on top of tall, often crooked stems. Use some of these to perpetuate the crop every fall.

WELCH ONIONS   P   18″   4   *Allium fistulosum*
Start from divisions in fall. Next fall harvest what you need, separate smaller bulbs from clumps and replant for new crop. Will self-sow.

ORANGE OSAGE [P] 6' 2 *Maclura pomifera*
Grows to forty feet in Texas and Arkansas, and makes a good tub plant
in winter up North if you have the room. A poor germinator, so sow
plenty of seed to insure one or two plants coming out of it.

*OREGANO P 24" 4 No botanical name

*PARSLEY B 8" 3 *Petroselinum hortense*

POKEROOT P 4' 2 *Phytolacca americana*
Also called POKEWEED.
Pinch off when twenty-four inches high to develop shorter, bushier plant.
Harvest berries to prevent self-sowing.

POPPY A 36" 2 *Papaver Rhoeas*
Not to be confused with opium poppy *(papaver somniferum)*, a perennial
which is illegal to grow in this country. Annual varieties produce more seed
than perennials, and so are more desirable in most herb gardens. Poppies
need more nourishment and moisture than the typical herb.

PYRETHRUM P 18" 2 *Chrysanthemum cinerariifolium*
Slow grower in first year, flowers appear second year, divide in spring of
third year.

RED VALERIAN P 3' 4 *Centranthus ruber*
Also called JUPITER'S BREAD.
Often confused with valerian (garden heliotrope) because of name, but
different plant. Compact grower, easily started from division. Flowers profusely in August.

ROQUETTE A 10" 3 *Eruca vesicaria sativa*
Also called ROCKET or RUGULA.
Quick and easy from seed. Harvest leaves when young and tender. Do not
permit to flower or leaves become tough and bitter. Resow several times
during season.

ROSE   P   5'   *Rosaceae*
It's possible to propagate roses from cuttings, but established plants in
every conceivable variety are so readily available that few gardeners will
want to go to that trouble. Unlike most herbs, rose bushes should be
heavily manured each fall to insure good production. Also you'll need some
pyrethrum spray to keep them insect-free during the season.

*ROSEMARY   [TP]   4'   5   *Rosmarinus officinalis*

WHITE ROSEMARY   [TP]   4'   5   *Rosmarinus officinalis Albus*
Grows exactly like officinalis, except produces white flowers, and stems on
new growth are very pale shade of green. Veteran herb gardeners can
recognize difference in the two plants before flowers appear.

ROSEMARY FORESTERI   [TP]   4'   5   *Rosmarinus officinalis Foresteri*
Strong growth pattern with broader, heavier leaves and stems than
officinalis has.

PINE SCENTED ROSEMARY   [TP]   2'   5   *Rosmarinus var.*
Compact grower with short leaves and stems, thin leaf pattern. One of
most manageable rosemarys to have indoors. Has strong pine flavor and
may be trained into miniature "Christmas tree" for the holidays if you
start in August.

PROSTRATE ROSEMARY   [TP]   6"   5   *Rosmarinus prostratus*
Excellent creeping plant for borders or rock gardens, but does best in
full sun. Bring inside, in a hanging basket to enjoy its profusion of tiny
blue blossoms in winter.

RUE   P   24"   2   *Ruta-graveolens*
Germinates quickly from seed—in five to seven days at 70 degrees. Trans-
plants easily. Pinch off flower stalks as they appear and plant will stay
more attractive and compact. Dig up and divide or replace with new plant

after third year to keep it from taking over area. Replace if plant becomes stalky and unattractive.

SAFFRON   P   8″   Bulb   *Crocus sativus*
Also called TRUE SAFFRON.
Takes three years to get flowers from seed, so buy bulbs in late summer or early fall. Plant four inches apart, pointy ends up (like garlic cloves). Lavender flowers with bright orange stigma appear in four to five weeks, and every fall thereafter. Dried stigma used for color and flavor—takes sixty thousand stigma to produce one pound of saffron.

SAFFLOWER   A   24″   2   *Carthamus tinctorius*
Also called FALSE SAFFRON, AMERICAN SAFFRON.
Large oval seeds sprout quickly and easily, but will become floppy if started too early indoors. Make sowing four weeks before date of setting out into garden. One of most attractive flowering herbs.

S A G E S

*SAGE   P   24″   5   *Salvia officinalis*
Also called GRAY SAGE, COMMON SAGE, GARDEN SAGE.

CLARY SAGE   B   4′   2   *Salvia Sclarea*
One of the tallest sages, has large silvery, fuzzy leaf and rosy blue or white flowers, which appear in second year. Self-sows readily if flowers are allowed to mature and drop seed. If started in garden in late summer will flower following year.

DWARF SAGE   [TP]   8″   5   *Salvia officinalis Compacta*
Miniature version of the basic culinary sage; useful in confined areas and patio planters. Best sage to pick for winter house plant—manageably small and has desired flavor.

GOLDEN SAGE   P   15"   5   *Salvia officinalis aurea*
Yellow-and-gray variegated leaf.

MEADOW SAGE   P   30"   2   *Salvia pratensis*
Big-leafed variety produces lovely spikes of blue flowers.

PINEAPPLE SAGE   TP   30"   5   *Salvia splendens*
Must be treated as annual up North, but well worth the trouble for its
splendid red flower and fragrant pineapple aroma. Growth stunted in cool
spring, but will shoot up once warm weather begins.

PURPLE SAGE   P   15"   5   *Salvia officinalis Purpurea*
Leaf comes in many shades of purple.

RED-TIPPED SAGE   A   15"   2   *Salvia viridis*
Also called RED-TOPPED SAGE.

TRI-COLOR SAGE   P   15"   5   *Salvia officinalis Tricolor*
Medium-sized hardy plant produces attractive gray, white and purple
variegated sages.

ST. JOHN'S WORT   P   18"   3   *Hypericum perforatum*
Keep confined by spading out perimeter growth in the fall and harvesting
flowers. If allowed to self-sow, it will spread like a weed.

SALAD BURNET. See BURNET.

GRAY SANTOLINA   P   12"   5   *Santolina Chamaecyparissus*
Also called LAVENDER COTTON.
Best grower of all the santolinas, can be trimmed or shaped into an attractive hedge or border. If untrimmed, produces pretty small yellow
flowers that look good in dried bouquets. Becomes overly woody and
should be replaced after four to five years.

PINNATA SANTOLINA   [P]   12″   5   *Santolina pinnata*
Small foliage, compact plant.

PRETTY CARROL SANTOLINA   [TP]   12″   5   *Santolina incana*
var. Pretty Carrol
Most attractive of gray santolinas has delicate, lacy foliage. May not survive very cold winters even if well mulched.

SAVORY. See SUMMER SAVORY, WINTER SAVORY.

SCENTED GERANIUMS

APPLE   [A]   12″   5   *Pelargonium odoratissimum*
Large light green soft leaves. Makes good hanging basket plant.

CINNAMON   [A]   18″   5   *Pelargonium quercifolium var.*
Sturdy, erect-growing plant.

COCONUT   [A]   15″   5   *Pelargonium grossularioides*
Small roundish leaves with distinctive dark markings that duplicate shape of edge of leaf and make plant easy to identify. Has trailing habit and looks good in hanging basket.

FRENCH LACE   [A]   18″   5   *Pelargonium crispum var.*
Erect grower like lemon crispum except has lovely cream-bordered leaves. Weaker lemon scent. Hardest to start from cuttings.

LEMON   [A]   24″   5   *Pelargonium limoneum*
Small, round crinkly leaves branch out from tall, sturdy stem.

LEMON CRISPUM   [A]   24″   5   *Pelargonium crispum*
Tinier lighter-colored leaves than lemon, not as bushy.

LIME   [A]   18″   5   *Pelargonium nervosum*
Small, roundish leaves. Grows like lemon only a little more compact.

MRS. KINGSLEY [A] 24″ 5 *Pelargonium rapaceum*
Rose-scented curly leaves. Periodic trimming will allow you to keep it from becoming too large in confined area.

MRS. TAYLOR [A] 24″ 5 *Pelargonium graveolens—Mrs. Taylor*
Rose-scented with deeply lobed leaves. One of the most popular varieties, easier to control than peppermint, rose or Mrs. K.

NUTMEG [A] 18″ 5 *Pelargonium fragrans*
Small grayish leaves, bushy growing pattern.

OLD SPICE [A] 18″ 5 *Pelargonium var.*
Grows like lemon, smells like after-shave.

PEPPERMINT A 24″ 5 *Pelargonium tomentosum*
Fastest grower and spreader with powerful peppermint aroma. Has large velvety, silver-green leaves. Too big to bring inside intact. In typical growing season will grow two to three times in breadth that of rose geranium, or about four feet across. To bring inside start new plant from cuttings in late summer.

PINE [A] 18″ 5 *Pelargonium denticulatum*
Bushy grower has narrow, lace-like leaves.

ROSE A 24″ 5 *Pelargonium graveolens*
Most popular of all scented geraniums; has irregularly lobed leaves, spreads to two feet across, but with more erect pattern than peppermint. Start from cuttings in late summer if you want this one indoors for winter.

SNOWFLAKE A 24″ 5 *Pelargonium capitatum—var.*
Strong bushy grower with round, deep green leaves with specks of white. To bring indoors, start new plant from cuttings in late summer. Pick sprig with most attractive color variation. What you see is what you will get.

SESAME   A   18″   2   *Sesamum indicum*
Also called BENE.
Very tender and needs long growing season—120 days—to produce the
desired seed, so must be started indoors up North. Harvest seed in late
summer or early fall. Don't plant out too early.

SHALLOTS   P   15″   Bulb   *Allium ascalonicum*
Plant from bulbs in fall or very early spring. Bulbs multiply into clumps,
which should be harvested after foliage dies down in late summer or early
fall. Replant small bulbs each year.

SILVER KING   P   24″   4   *Artemesia ludoviciana*
Cultivate regularly to keep fungus from forming at base of plant. Spreads
rapidly, so subdivide in early spring every other year after second growing
season.

SILVER MOUND   P   6″   4   *Artemesia var.*
Develops into a stunning solid mound-shaped mass of lacy, silvery leaves.
Shaped as it is, little air circulation reaches base of plant, so it is extremely
susceptible to rot during wet weather. If this happens, cut back the dead
parts and plant will revive, though it may not re-establish its attractive
form in the same season.

SILVER QUEEN   P   24″   4   *Artemesia var.*
Slightly broader leaf than silver king and tends to grow shorter and
showier. Requires same care as its mate.

SORREL   P   18″   3   *Rumex scutatus*
Also called FRENCH SORREL.
Self-sows readily so keep harvesting or it will crowd out other herbs.
Early in second year keep cutting flower stalks as they appear. Remove
crop and replant from new seed in third year, otherwise it gets too big
and its leaves too tough.

SOUTHERNWOOD   P   3'   4   *Artemesia Abrotanum*
Also called OLD MAN.
Easily started from divisions in early spring. Sprigs and branches can be
harvested twice during growing season for use in bouquets and dried arrangements. Erect grower, keeps good shape. Subdivide every spring after
second year.

*SUMMER SAVORY   A   18"   3   *Satureja hortensis*

SWEET CICELY   P   3'   4   *Myrrhis odorata*
Nearly impossible to start from seed. Likes partial shade. Develops heavy
root systems that should be divided in early spring after third year. Don't
confuse with the wild American sweet cicely *(Osmorhiza longistylis)*,
which grows freely in many northern wooded areas.

SWEET MYRTLE   [TP]   18"   5   *Myrtus communis compacta*
Takes patience to start from cutting, but once established easy to grow.
Tiny glossy leaves produce a pleasant, spicy scent when rubbed together.
If bringing indoors as a house plant in the fall, cut back slightly—as you
would for rosemary.

SWEET WOODRUFF   P   12"   4/5   *Galium odoratum*
Division best way to propagate. Nearly impossible from seed, and cuttings
take well only if protected from hot sun while rooting. If starting from
cutting, locate rooting medium in filtered sunlight and keep moist. The
established plant likes a cool, shady, moist spot in the garden—don't let
it dry out in summer drought or you'll lose it. Makes excellent spreading
ground cover.

TANSY   P   36"   4   *Tanacetum vulgare*
Simple from division in early spring—but gets too big topside to do so
safely any later. Its aggressive root system needs plenty of room and oc-
casional composting or manuring. Subdivide after second growing season
and each year thereafter to keep confined.

FERN-LEAF TANSY   P   24"   4   *Tanacetum vulgare crispum*
A smaller, less rapid-growing version of tansy, considered more attractive because of its fern-like leaf, though it will not produce as many flowers. Subdivide after second season and every other year thereafter.

*TARRAGON   P   30"   4   *Artemesia Dracunculus*

TEUCRIUM GERMANDER   P   15"   5   *Teucrium Chamaedrys*
Easy from cuttings. Lends itself to shaping into small shiny-leafed hedges similar to boxwood, so popular in border plantings. Very hardy, but don't trim late in season or it may lose vitality in some areas during a severe winter (as happens to boxwood).

THYMES

THYME   P   12"   1   *Thymus vulgaris*
Also called ENGLISH THYME, COMMON THYME.

CARAWAY THYME   P   1"   4   *Thymus Herba-barona*
Low creeping variety spreads rapidly. Divide every two or three years. Very different caraway fragrance.

GERMAN THYME   P   12"   1   *Thymus vulgaris var.*
Treat exactly as Thyme. More compact growing habit.

GOLDEN THYME   [P]   8"   5   *Thymus aureus*
A slow spreader better started from cuttings which should be picked for best variegation and color. Makes good pot plant if brought indoors to a cool, sunny window. Often used to shape into bonsai plants. Develops a redness in stems in coolness of early spring.

LEMON THYME   P   4"   4   *Thymus citriodorus*
Rapid spreader needs division every two or three years. Has strong lemony

flavor, but will revert and lose scent if cross-pollination with other varieties occurs, so keep flowers trimmed.

ORANGE BALSAM THYME　　　P　　　8″　　　5　　　*Thymus var.*
Compact growers with citrus flavor.

OREGANO THYME　　　P　　　8″　　　5　　　*Thymus var.*
Spreads slowly so not easy to start from division.

PINK THYME　　　P　　　1–3″　　　4　　　*Thymus Serpyllum roseus*
Exactly like red except for color of blossoms.

RED THYME　　　P　　　1–3″　　　4　　　*Thymus Serpyllum splendens*
Similar to white except grows taller, less compactly. Has darker foliage and red blossoms.

SILVER THYME　　　[P]　　　8″　　　5　　　*Thymus citriodorus argenteus*
Similar to golden except grows more erect.

COMMON SILVER THYME　　[P]　　8″　　5　　*Thymus vulgaris variegata*
More distinct variegation in leaves than silver thyme. Pick your cuttings for best color pattern.

WHITE-FLOWERING THYME　　P　　1″　　4　　*Thymus Serpyllum albus*
Lowest-growing thyme. Has light green foliage, grows thickly and spreads quickly. Tiny white flowers appear in June. Best variety for filling in between flagstones or bricks in walkways.

WOOLLY THYME　　　P　　　1″　　　4　　　*Thymus lanuginosus*
Fuzzy, blue-gray foliage, rapid spreader, and easily divided, but most prone to rot of all the thymes, so do not plant where taller plants will shade it and do not mulch for winter.

TOBACCO   A   5'   2   *Nicotiana Tabacum*
Easy from seed but rapid grower, so do not start indoors any sooner than four to five weeks before date of setting out in garden. Needs plenty of room, richer soil and more moisture than most herbs.

TORMENTIL   P   6"   3/4   *Potentilla Tormentilla*
Hardy, rapid low-growing spreader; needs regular attention after second year to keep confined. Yellow flowers, fine-textured leaves. Harvest flowers before they mature to prevent self-sowing. Divide in spring of every year to keep confined.

VALERIAN   P   3'   4   *Valeriana officinalis*
Also called GARDEN HELIOTROPE, PERENNIAL HELIOTROPE.
Will flower at end of first season, every August thereafter. Subdivide after the second growing season and every other year thereafter. Benefits from annual manuring or composting.

VERVAIN   P   24"   2   *Verbena officinalis*
Bushy grower. Pick off its small purplish flowers or it will self-sow widely. Divide every other year.

VIOLETS   P   4"   3/4   *Viola odorata*
Does better in partial shade and needs fairly rich soil. Subdivide every third year or plants will become too crowded.

WATER CRESS   B   3"   1   *Nasturtium officinale*
Start indoors in peat pots. Seeds sprout in two weeks, thereafter growth is rapid. Plant in shallow brook of fresh, unpolluted water in spots protected from full force of running water—use stones if necessary to blunt stream. Begin harvest within two to three weeks and keep harvesting until brook runs dry.

WELD   A   24"   3   *Reseda luteola*
Slow grower does fairly well in partial shade; start from seed in peat pots to reduce shock of transplant.

WINTER SAVORY   P   12"   2   *Satureja montana*
Very slow from seed—must be started indoors at least four months before setting out. Has a compact, shrub-like growing habit and needs regular trimming. Normally hardy but will winterkill in very wet conditions. May become overly woody and need replacement in four to five years.

WOAD   B   36"   3   *Isatis tinctoria*
Does not flower until second year; cut blossoms promptly to prevent fierce self-sowing.

WORMWOOD   P   24"   2/4   *Artemisia Absinthium*
Transplants well after being started from seed even though it has a large and fast-growing tap root. Subdivide every other year.

ROMAN WORMWOOD   P   18"   4   *Artemisia pontica*
Divide every other year to prevent overly heavy growth. Prone to fungus problems in damp weather.

YARROW (red)   P   24"   2/4   *Achillea Millefolium*

YARROW (yellow)   P   24"   2/4   *Achillea filipendulina*
Seeds available but hard to get to sprout. Still, if interested in specific color, it's sometimes better to go by the seed than by guesses about what color flowers your neighbor's yarrow will produce. Needs a bit more moisture than average herbs. Divide after second growing season and every other year thereafter.

Harvesting & Storing
The 15 Basic Herbs

INFORMATION SUPPLIED HERE is limited primarily to special harvesting and storing techniques for each of the fifteen basic culinary herbs. These are applicable to many of the herbs featured in the other garden plans, too.

BASIL   Cut sprigs or leaves as needed, beginning six weeks after plants first appear. Pinch out flowering tops whenever they appear.

For saving: Freeze in recipe-sized portions, or hang to dry in small bunches in a dark place. Basil darkens readily in too much heat, so be extra careful if oven-drying. Once it becomes brittle, strip leaves from stems and store in jars. Or crumble them with your fingers, or pass them through a coarse sieve, before storing.

To preserve basil in vinegar, force several fresh sprigs into a store-bought bottle of white vinegar and let stand out of the light for two or three weeks. You end up with two products for off-season use—basil-flavored vinegar and the basil leaves themselves, which can be extracted, rinsed and used as fresh. The dark opal variety turns the vinegar pleasantly pink.

Remember to make your final harvest of basil before the first 40-degree night, or this very tender plant might be lost.

BAY In first year, pick out center, then harvest sparingly, selecting leaves around base of plant so as to allow this slow grower to develop properly.

For saving: We suggest bringing your bay plant inside in its pot for the winter. If you do that, you don't have to worry about storing the harvest. However, bay is easily dried for winter use, too. Spread leaves in a single layer on a tray and leave in a warm dark room for a week or two, with a board or book on top of the leaves to keep them from curling. Or oven-dry the leaves in a slow oven.

Put the crisp leaves through a coffee grinder or your blender, on the coarse/chop setting, then store. That way you'll be able to use the much stronger-flavored dried bay in your cooking with discretion.

CHERVIL Cut the lacy leaves as needed, beginning eight weeks after plants first appear. Cut from the outside of the plant so it keeps growing up and out from the center.

For saving: A lot of cooks don't think chervil is worth drying because its small leaf gets even smaller in the process and, they say, its delicate flavor is practically negligible in the dry state.

But see what you think. Harvest before flowering, place in thin layers and dry on trays in a good spot or in your oven, then store.

CHIVES Take small bunches from each plant rather than giving a crew-cut to one plant all at once. Cut it down to about two inches and the plant will come back several times in one season. Also, you'll see more attractive purple flowers per clump around July.

For saving: Harvest as above, but get rid of the yellow and tough shoots, then chop into one to two-inch lengths and spread on a tray or screen and dry quickly in an oven.

Some people think you get more flavor freezing chives than you do drying them. In preparation for freezing, wash the chives, pat them dry, eliminate poor-looking ones. Then chop and store in plastic bags in the freezer.

CORIANDER If you're growing coriander primarily for its *leaves* (sold as Chinese parsley or cilantro in Oriental or Spanish markets), harvest as needed, beginning eight weeks after plants first appear.

If you're growing it for the *seeds,* then let plants mature, harvesting leaves sparingly if you wish. In late summer, harvest seedheads after the first seeds have turned brown. Then hang seedheads upside-down in your drying spot and let the rest of the seed ripen. Place a clean tray or like container immediately beneath the bunch to catch the seed as it falls—if the seed falls from a greater height, it will bounce all over the place. That's why some people prefer to catch it in paper bags. Anyway, store the collected seed as is—don't crush or grind it.

DILL The foliage can be lightly harvested throughout the growing season, beginning six weeks after plants first appear. Don't cut too deeply, though, or you'll hamper development of the umbels, or seedheads. Best flavor in leaf is at time of flowering.

For saving: The seedheads should be cut after the first seeds have turned brown, just as with coriander. Hang them upside-down in a good spot and let the seed drop on a tray or in a bag as it matures. Or dry it in a slow oven before storing.

Use the seed to make dill vinegar, or store in airtight jars in a dark place. The dried seed will keep its flavor for several years.

The foliage on dill plants can be saved, too. At the end of season, after taking seedheads and before foliage turns brown, harvest, wash, pat dry and store the leaves in plastic bags in the freezer. Or dry them in bunches and then strip the leaves for storage. Or chop them first and then dry on trays or in the oven.

If a few seedheads do mature on the plant and fall to the ground, they might survive under a winter mulch and show up as volunteers the following spring.

OREGANO   Cut sprigs and leaves in about four to six weeks, or as soon as a good growth pattern has been established. In the first year, this would be about when the plant has reached six inches in height and six inches across. In succeeding years, wait until plant has produced four to six inches in new growth, in the spring.

For saving: Harvest within four inches of the ground every month, and hang in bunches in a dry, dark place. Some gardeners prefer to wait until flowers appear before harvesting, but don't get as much foliage harvest if they do.

PARSLEY In first year, begin cutting eight to ten weeks after plants first appear. Harvest as needed, cutting to within three to four inches off the ground.

In second year, begin cutting as soon as new growth appears.

For saving: Cut the plants down by half at midsummer. Take final harvest after first light frost in fall.

Some cooks think frozen parsley has a better flavor than dried parsley. It needs to be washed, patted dry, chopped and then frozen in freezer bags. Don't thaw before using as it will come out limp.

To dry, hang in small bunches or lay out thinly and process in a slow oven. Then crush it or put it through a coarse sieve before storing.

ROSEMARY Harvest fresh sprigs as needed. Don't cut into woody parts (as will develop after second year) or you could hinder development of the plant.

For saving: Dry sprigs on a tray or screen—they'll look like pine needles when finished. Then chop coarsely in a blender or coffee grinder and store.

SAGE Cut leaves and sprigs as needed once plant begins to grow vigorously in the garden. In the first year, this may not be until mid- or even late summer. In succeeding years, you can begin the harvest just as soon as new tender growth appears on the bush.

For saving: Cut six to eight inches top growth two to four times per year, after the first year.

Sage can be dried in small bunches or in thin layers. Its

tougher leaf usually requires a bit more time for adequate drying than any of the other basic herbs.

SPEARMINT   Cut sprigs and leaves as needed. This is one herb you don't have to be fussy about in harvesting, even in its first years in your garden. It will grow no matter how you treat it.

For saving: Harvest at the onset of flowering—you should be able to get several harvests in one season.

Always handle mint with care—like tarragon, its leaves bruise easily.

Hang in small bunches or lay out in thin layers and dry in slow oven, then strip leaves and store in jars.

Spearmint can be crushed before storing but peppermint— the mint preferred for teas—is better left in leaf form and used that way in making infusions (see Tea Garden notes in Plans Section).

SUMMER SAVORY   Make first picking of tender new shoots about six weeks after plants first appear, or when they are four to six inches high. Then they'll begin to grow vigorously and within four to five weeks you should be able to harvest regularly as needed. It's a much more prolific grower than its hardier cousin, winter savory, and under average conditions you should be able to harvest from it every other week throughout the growing season if you don't cut it too far back at any one time.

For saving: Cut leafy tops at budding time. Leaves get noticeably darker after blossoming and are not as attractive to dry and store. Hang in small bunches or dry on trays, then strip leaves for storage.

MARJORAM   Harvest leaves and sprigs as needed in the first year, beginning four to six weeks after transplant into the garden. After the first year, you can make a good picking of marjoram, as of summer savory and oregano, nearly every other week in the growing season. Make your final harvest after the first frost.

For saving: Cut, wash, bunch-dry in a good spot or oven-dry with care. Strip free of stems and debris and store.

TARRAGON Cut fresh leaves as needed beginning about six to eight weeks after transplant into the garden in the first year—this herb takes a bit longer to get established than the other perennials. Once it has a good growth pattern, when it is about six to eight inches across, you can harvest selectively.

After the first year, cut to within 6 inches of the ground as needed every month in the growing season.

For saving: Handle tarragon leaves carefully; like mint leaves, they bruise easily and lose their aroma. Dry in bunches or on trays. For vinegar, cut four or five stems and stick in a bottle of white vinegar, then cap and store for a couple of weeks in a cool dark area, such as a cupboard or cabinet.

THYME In the first year, cut sprigs beginning six weeks from date of transplant, but don't harvest too intensively or too deeply. In succeeding years you can take more of it and more often, but avoid cutting into woody stems. Make a final cut after the first frost.

For saving: Cut six inches of leafy tops and flower clusters before flowers actually appear. It's easy to dry thyme on trays or screens because it doesn't hold that much moisture to begin with. When it becomes brittle, strip the leaves or process it through a coarse sieve, then store.

PART V

Appendixes

Culinary uses of the 15 basic herbs

The following is a somewhat informal, selective list of suggestions for using the herbs featured in our basic culinary garden. Follow our recommendations, consult your favorite cookbooks, and experiment.

BASIL
fish, and game, such as duck or
    venison
omelettes
pesto sauce
tomatoes, tomato soups or sauces
almost all cold salads

BAY (LEAVES)
bouquet garni
marinades
sauces, stocks and stuffings
stews and meat pies

CHERVIL
chicken
cream or cottage cheese
green vegetables, such as spinach,
    or green salads
omelettes
soups, and cream or tomato sauces
veal

CHIVES
cream or cottage cheese
green salads
omelettes
any soups or sauces calling for a
    mild onion flavor
essential as a garnish for
    vichyssoise

CORIANDER (LEAVES)
chicken or pea soups
guacamole
roasts
stews

CORIANDER (SEEDS)
apple pie
chili dishes or curries
ginger bread

DILL (LEAVES)
chicken, fish or veal
green beans or salads (particularly
    cucumber)
boiled or sautéed potatoes and
    potato salads
sour cream or butter sauces

DILL (SEEDS)
cole slaw
pickles
sauerkraut

OREGANO
pizza
tomato salads or tomato sauces

PARSLEY
bouquet garni
chicken or fish
boiled or sautéed potatoes
salads

PARSLEY (cont.)
soups, stews and stocks
as a garnish for almost any cooked
    meat or vegetable

ROSEMARY
chicken, fish or almost any game
    bird, such as duck or partridge
almost any meat such as beef,
    lamb or pork
marinades
poultry stuffings and savory biscuits
spinach

SAGE
cheese and cheese spreads
chowders
strong-flavored meats, such as duck,
    goose or rabbit
pork and sausage
poultry stuffings

MINT
cream cheeses
chocolate
fruit dishes
green salads and vegetables, such as
    peas and zucchini
jellies
juleps
lamb or veal
boiled or sautéed potatoes
teas
yogurt sauces or soups

SUMMER SAVORY
hot or cold beans or lentils

deviled eggs or omelettes
fat-fleshed fish
meat loaves
pork roasts
potatoes
tomatoes

SWEET MARJORAM
to flavor beans, carrots, peas,
    potatoes and tomato dishes
chicken, goose, lamb and pork
minestrone and mock turtle soup
salads
sausages and stews
sauces and stuffings

TARRAGON
chicken, fish and veal
egg dishes
poultry stuffings
salads and salad dressings
Béarnaise, mustard and tartar
    sauces

THYME
bouquet garni
chicken, fish and veal
Creole and gumbo dishes
marinades
hearty meat stews and pies
mutton, pork and rabbit
stocks, and soups, such as bisques
    or chowders
poultry stuffings

Here are the addresses of the headquarters of the Extension Service in each state. Write to the main office in your state for helpful literature on home herb gardening. Also ask for a copy of a general list of publications available, and for information on soil-testing.

ALABAMA
Auburn University
Auburn, Alabama 36830

ALASKA
University of Alaska
Fairbanks, Alaska 99701

ARIZONA
University of Arizona
Tucson, Arizona 85721

ARKANSAS
Post Office Box 391
Little Rock, Arkansas 72203

CALIFORNIA
University of California
2200 University Avenue
Berkeley, California 94720

COLORADO
Colorado State University
Fort Collins, Colorado 80521

CONNECTICUT
University of Connecticut
Storrs, Connecticut 06268

DELAWARE
University of Delaware
Newark, Delaware 19711

DISTRICT OF COLUMBIA
Federal City College
1424 K. Street, N.W.
Washington, D.C. 20005

FLORIDA
University of Florida
Gainesville, Florida 32611

GEORGIA
University of Georgia
Athens, Georgia 30601

HAWAII
University of Hawaii
Honolulu, Hawaii 96822

IDAHO
University of Idaho
Morrill Hall
Moscow, Idaho 83843

ILLINOIS
University of Illinois
Urbana, Illinois 61801

INDIANA
Purdue University
Lafayette, Indiana 47907

IOWA
Iowa State University
Ames, Iowa 50010

KANSAS
Kansas State University
Manhattan, Kansas 66506

KENTUCKY
University of Kentucky
Lexington, Kentucky 40506

LOUISIANA
Louisiana State University
Baton Rouge, Louisiana 70803

MAINE
University of Maine
Orono, Maine 04473

MARYLAND
University of Maryland
College Park, Maryland 20742

MASSACHUSETTS
University of Massachusetts
Amherst, Massachusetts 01002

MICHIGAN
Michigan State University
East Lansing, Michigan 48823

MINNESOTA
University of Minnesota
St. Paul Minnesota, 55101

MISSISSIPPI
Mississippi State University
Mississippi State, Mississippi 39762

MISSOURI
University of Missouri
309 University Hall
Columbia, Missouri 65201

MONTANA
Montana State University
Bozeman, Montana 59715

NEBRASKA
University of Nebraska
Lincoln, Nebraska 68508

NEVADA
University of Nevada
Reno, Nevada 89507

NEW HAMPSHIRE
University of New Hampshire
Taylor Hall
Durham, New Hampshire 03824

NEW JERSEY
Rutgers—The State University
P.O. Box 231
New Brunswick, New Jersey 08903

NEW MEXICO
New Mexico State University
Las Cruces, New Mexico 88001

NEW YORK
New York State College of Agriculture
Ithaca, New York 14853

NORTH CAROLINA
North Carolina State University
Raleigh, North Carolina 27607

NORTH DAKOTA
North Dakota State University
Fargo, North Dakota 58102

OHIO
Ohio State University
2120 Fyffe Road
Columbus, Ohio 43210

OKLAHOMA
Oklahoma State University
Stillwater, Oklahoma 74074

OREGON
Oregon State University
Corvallis, Oregon 97331

PENNSYLVANIA
Pennsylvania State University
University Park, Pennsylvania 16802

PUERTO RICO
University of Puerto Rico
Rio Piedras, Puerto Rico 00928

RHODE ISLAND
University of Rhode Island
Kingston, Rhode Island 02881

SOUTH CAROLINA
Clemson University
Clemson, South Carolina 29631

SOUTH DAKOTA
South Dakota State University
Brookings, South Dakota 57006

TENNESSEE
University of Tennessee
P.O. Box 1071
Knoxville, Tennessee 37901

TEXAS
Texas A & M University
College Station, Texas 77843

UTAH
Utah State University
Logan, Utah 84321

VERMONT
University of Vermont
Burlington, Vermont 05401

VIRGINIA
Virginia Polytechnic
Institute and State University
Blacksburg, Virginia 24061

VIRGIN ISLANDS
P.O. Box 166 Kingshill
St. Croix, Virgin Islands 00850

WASHINGTON
Washington State University
Pullman, Washington 99163

WEST VIRGINIA
West Virginia University
294 Coliseur
Morgantown, Virginia 26505

WISCONSIN
University of Wisconsin
432 North Lake Street
Madison, Wisconsin 53706

WYOMING
University of Wyoming
Box 3354, University Station
Laramie, Wyoming 82070

"START-FROM-SCRATCH" SCHEDULE

This schedule for starting a basic culinary garden is based on an average date of last frost in the spring of *May 10* and an average date of first frost in the fall of *October 10*. Gardeners in areas of the country with different frost dates can adapt the schedule simply by determining their own frost dates and working from there.

GROUP 1

Cluster Sowing Indoors

	sow seed	at 70°, seed germinates in	move to cooler place (50°–60°)	pinch out tops	transplant to garden	begin to harvest
CHIVES	Feb. 15	3–5 days	March 1	——	April 20	June 1
MARJORAM	"	5–7 days	"	April 1	May 1	"
THYME	"	3–5 days	"	"	April 20	"

GROUP 2

Spot Sowing Indoors

	sow seed	at 70°, seed germinates in	move to cooler place (60°–65°)	pinch out tops	transplant to garden	begin to harvest
BASIL	March 30	7–10 days	May 1	May 1	May 25	July 1
CHERVIL	March 15	"	April 15	—	May 10	June 15
CORIANDER	"	5–7 days	"	—	"	"

GROUP 3

Cluster Sowing Outdoors

	set out containers to warm soil	sow seed	seed germinates in	remove plastic covers	remove containers	pinch tops	begin to harvest
DILL	May 10	May 15	5–7 days	June 1	June 10	—	July 1
PARSLEY	May 1	May 5	10–15 days	"	"	—	"
SUMMER SAVORY	May 10	May 15	5–7 days	"	"	June 10	"

GROUP 4

Making Divisions of Spreading Perennials

	make division and plant	pinch tops	begin to harvest
MINT	April 15	May 15	June 15
OREGANO	"	"	"
TARRAGON	"	"	"

GROUP 5

Taking Cuttings of Single-Stem Perennials

	make cutting	at 70° roots form in	transplant into pots	pinch tops	put into cool-off place	transplant to garden	begin to harvest	bring in for winter
BAY	Dec. 1– Jan. 1	6–8 weeks	March 1	May 1 or 6" high	May 1	May 10	late summer	Oct. 10
ROSEMARY	Feb. 1	2–3 weeks	"	April 1	April 15	"	midsummer	"
SAGE	Feb. 1	2–3 weeks	"	"	"	"	"	—

SOURCES OF HERB SEED

Here is a list of reputable and generally dependable sources of herb seed and, in some cases, of herb plants. Firms I have personally done business with are marked with an asterisk.

*W. Atlee Burpee Co.
Philadelphia, Pa. 19132
Clinton, Iowa 52732
Riverside, Calif. 92502

*Carrol Gardens
444 E. Main St.
Box 310
Westminster, Md.. 21157

*Joseph Harris Co.
Moreton Farm
Rochester, N.Y. 14624

*Howe Hill Herbs
Howe Hill Road
Camden, Maine 04843

Kilgore Seed Co.
Sanford, Fla. 32771

*Le Jardin du Gourmet
Box 5, Route 15
West Danville, Vt. 05873

*Meadowbrook Herb Garden
Wyoming, R.I. 02898

Nichols Garden Nursery
1190 North Pacific Highway
Albany, Oregon 97321

*North Central Comfrey Producers
Box 195
Glidden, Wis. 54527

*Geo. W. Park Seed Co.
Cokesbury Road
Greenwood, S.C. 29647

*Otto Richter & Sons, Ltd.
Box 26
Goodwood, Ontario
Canada L0C 1A0

Rocky Hollow Herb Farm
Box 354
Sussex, N.J. 07461

*Stokes Seeds
Stokes Building
Buffalo, N.Y. 14240

Sunnybrook Farms Nursery
9448 Mayfield Rd.
Chesterland, Ohio 44026

*Taylor's Garden, Inc.
1535 Lone Oak Rd.
Vista, Calif. 92083

Thompson & Morgan, Inc.
Box 100
Farmingdale, N.J. 07727

Vita Green Farms
Box 878
Vista, Calif. 92083

Wyatt Quarles Seed Co.
Box 2131
Raleigh, N.C. 27602

*Yankee Peddler Herb Farm
Highway 36–N
Brenham, Tex. 77833

Index